A Handbook for Literacy INSTRUCTIONAL and ASSESSMENT STRATEGIES, K–8

A Handbook for Literacy
INSTRUCTIONAL and ASSESSMENT STRATEGIES, K–8

Patricia A. Antonacci
Iona College

Catherine M. O'Callaghan
Iona College

Boston • New York • San Francisco
Mexico City • Montreal • Toronto • London • Madrid • Munich • Paris
Hong Kong • Singapore • Tokyo • Cape Town • Sydney

Senior Series Editor: Aurora Martínez Ramos
Series Editorial Assistant: Kevin Shannon
Senior Marketing Manager: Krista Clark
Production Editor: Annette Joseph
Editorial-Production Service: Omegatype Typography, Inc.
Composition Buyer: Linda Cox
Manufacturing Buyer: Andrew Turso
Electronic Composition: Omegatype Typography, Inc.
Interior Design: Carol Somberg
Cover Administrator: Joel Gendron

For related titles and support materials, visit our online catalog at
www.ablongman.com.

Between the time website information is gathered and then published, it is not
unusual for some sites to have closed. Also, the transcription of URLs can result
in typographical errors. The publisher would appreciate notification where these
errors occur so that they may be corrected in subsequent editions.

Many of the designations used by manufacturers and sellers to distinguish their
products are claimed as trademarks. Where those designations appear in this book,
and Allyn and Bacon was aware of a trademark claim, the designations have been
printed in initial or all caps.

Library of Congress Cataloging-in-Publication Data

Antonacci, Patricia.
    A handbook for literacy instructional and assessment strategies, K–8 / Patricia A.
Antonacci, Catherine M. O'Callaghan. — 1st ed.
      p. cm.
    Includes bibliographical references and index.
    ISBN 0-205-42217-9
    1. Language arts (Elementary)—Handbooks, manuals, etc.   2. Language arts
(Elementary)—Ability testing—Handbooks, manuals, etc. I. O'Callaghan, Catherine
M. II. Title.
  LB1576.A627   2006
  372.6—dc22

                                      2005047444

Printed in the United States of America

10 9 8 7 6 5 4 3 2 1   09 08 07 06 05

This handbook is dedicated to our nieces and nephews,
who are beginning their journeys to become literate.

Catherine's young family:
James and Mary Anne

Patricia's young family:
Brittney, Matthew, Michael, and Sean

CONTENTS

SECTION **3**

Instructional and Assessment Strategies for Developing WRITING   89

SECTION **4**

Instructional and Assessment Strategies for Developing DISCUSSION SKILLS   139

SECTION 5

Instructional and Assessment Strategies for Developing CRITICAL THINKING 165

The purpose of *A Handbook for Literacy Instructional and Assessment Strategies, K–8* is to provide a resource for literacy instruction for busy classroom teachers in kindergarten through grade 8. This handbook also offers students in teacher-preparation programs a reserve of the best literacy strategies used by teachers in elementary and middle schools, serving as a companion to the traditional literacy textbook. The significance of monitoring students' literacy development and providing documentation for reporting the results of their performances is demonstrated by the prominent role we have given to classroom assessment tools within the strategies. Each instructional strategy is aligned with an assessment tool that facilitates the teacher's assessing and documenting students' progress using classroom performances that are part of the literacy program.

How to Use This Handbook

To simplify the use of this handbook, each strategy is organized in the same way: (a) the instructional context, (b) the framework or background information, (c) learner outcomes, (d) the instructional procedure, (e) an application, (f) the assessment procedure, and (g) professional resources and references.

The thirty-five strategies in this handbook are grouped by target literacy-learning areas. For example, when a teacher is looking for a strategy that emphasizes comprehension instruction, he or she would look in Section One, Comprehension, which contains instruc tional and assessment strategies for teaching comprehension skills. Although each strategy integrates a variety of literacy skills, one skill is targeted.

The *instructional context* is presented at the beginning of each strategy. By reviewing an easy-to-read table organized around (a) grade levels, (b) literacy levels, (c) group sizes, (d) literature genres, and (e) literacy skills, the teacher may quickly decide whether a given strategy is appropriate for a particular group of students. Here is a sample chart that illustrates the instructional context for a particular strategy:

INSTRUCTIONAL CONTEXT				
Grade Level	**Literacy Level**	**Group Size**	**Literature Genre**	**Literacy Skills**
○ K–1	○ Emergent	● Whole class	● Fiction	❖ Comprehension
● 2–4	● Early	● 8–10 students	○ Nonfiction	● Vocabulary
● 5–6	● Transitional	○ 4–6 students		● Discussion
○ 7–8	○ Fluent	○ Individual		● Writing
				● Critical thinking

● *Applicable*	○ *Not applicable*	❖ *Target skill*

This chart depicts a strategy that is appropriate for grades 2–4 and 5–6 for students at the early and transitional stages of literacy. The strategy would be best applied with the whole class or with a group of 8–10 students using fiction. The column *"Literacy Skills,"* shows that all of the skill areas are utilized by students; however, comprehension is the target area of instruction and assessment, as depicted with a starshaped bullet. The codes for the applicability of each area within the instructional context for the strategy are identified below the chart. As the teacher becomes proficient using the strategy, he or she may modify it to change one or more of the recommendations offered here.

Key Features

- Instructional strategies are organized into five sections denoting important literacy skills typically developed in elementary classrooms, and the strategies are alphabetized within each section.
- For each instructional strategy, the appropriate literacy levels and grade levels are indicated.
- Assessment tools that offer teachers the option to monitor and document student progress throughout the school year are aligned with the instructional strategies.
- Each instructional strategy and assessment tool is presented in a step-by-step approach for on-the-spot use by busy classroom teachers, reading specialists, and staff developers. This step-by-step approach will also help novice teachers develop their craft by systematically organizing their instruction.
- Suggestions for modifying instructional and assessment strategies for English language learners and students with special needs are offered throughout this handbook.
- Professional resources are offered at the end of each instructional strategy to assist readers in further understanding the approaches.
- Samples of student work as well as graphic organizers are included in each section.

Acknowledgments

We wish to thank all of the practicing teachers within our literacy program at Iona College who tried out the instructional strategies and assessment tools in their classrooms and offered us valuable feedback. We also extend our appreciation to the teacher candidates who tutored students in their field experiences and asked insightful questions related to the use of the instructional approaches. Our gratitude goes to our reviewers, as well: Bruce A. Gutknecht, University of North Florida, and Sara Rung-Pulte, Northern Kentucky University. Their suggestions were extremely helpful.

Finally, we are especially indebted to the wonderful team of editors at Allyn & Bacon who were responsible for this project from beginning to end. A special thanks to our editor, Aurora Martinez, who took the time to share her expertise with us.

Instructional and Assessment Strategies for Developing COMPREHENSION

Within this section are strategies to help students develop their comprehension skills. Although the emphasis is on comprehension instruction and assessment, students will be involved in using other forms of language to complete each activity.

CHARACTER HAND PORTRAITS

A Strategy for Developing Comprehension of Narrative Text

INSTRUCTIONAL CONTEXT				
Grade Level	Literacy Level	Group Size	Literature Genre	Literacy Skills
● K–1	● Emergent	● Whole class	● Fiction	❖ Comprehension
● 2–4	● Early	● 8–10 students	○ Nonfiction	● Vocabulary
● 5–6	● Transitional	○ 4–6 students		● Discussion
○ 7–8	○ Fluent	○ Individual		● Writing
				● Critical thinking

● Applicable	○ Not applicable	❖ Target skill

A Framework for Instruction

Character Hand Portraits may be used to help children understand how an author develops a character in a narrative text. Students create hand portraits that illustrate a character's traits and biographical information. The students also choose symbols to represent the character displayed on their hand portraits.

Literature opens up the world for children to explore. Literature-based programs help children to develop facility with language as they hear new vocabulary words and see new writing structures (Galda & Cullinan, 2002). The shift toward literature-based programs began in the 1980s in response to Rosenblatt's (1978) transactional theory of literary response.

Rosenblatt stated that the reader constructs meaning by interacting with the text. The reader approaches each book or story in a particular way, or what Rosenblatt termed *stance*. An *efferent stance* is when the reader is seeking information, as in the reading of a textbook or phone book. When the reader takes an *aesthetic stance*, the goal is to produce a personal response to the book or story. When students engage in literature circles, the focus of the discussion is their literary response.

Research on literature-based programs has demonstrated its positive effects on children's print awareness and word recognition skills (Reutzel, Oda, & Moore, 1989). In one study, as children listened or read quality literature, their knowledge of written language improved (Purcell-Gates, McIntyre, & Freppon, 1995). Students in literature-based programs have also shown improvements in their vocabulary and reading comprehension (Reutzel & Cooter, 1990). Clearly, literature-based programs can lead to improvements in literacy skills when students explore and respond to quality children's literature.

Learner Outcomes

- The students will describe a character's traits as well as actions.
- The students will use evidence from the story to defend the character traits they have described.
- The students will create Character Hand Portraits after reading a narrative text.

Instructional Procedure

Before beginning the story, the teacher solicits students' predictions regarding the story content based on the picture clues and title of the story. The teacher records the students' predictions on a chart for future reference and then begins the strategy.

Step by Step

1. The teacher begins the guided reading of the story by asking the students, "What do you think is going to happen to the main character?" The teacher records the students' predictions on chart paper.

2. After the students have reached the midpoint or critical event in the story, the teacher asks them to brainstorm and complete the graphic organizer shown in Figure 1.1. The students may work on this in pairs or in small groups.

3. The students bring their graphic organizers to the discussion group and must support their responses with evidence from the story. The teacher should allow sufficient time for all students to provide at least one response in each column.

4. After discussion, each pair or group completes a character web that lists the traits of the main character of the story (see Figure 1.2).

After the Story

1. After the students have completed reading the story, they review their character web and discuss changes in the character's traits. The teacher observes the interaction and responses of the students during the discussion period.

2. After finalizing their list of character traits, the students are ready to make Character Hand Portraits. The teacher hands out pieces of large paper as well as crayons, markers, and other art supplies.

Name of Character _____			
What did the character do?	**What did the character say?**	**What did the character think?**	**What did the character feel?**

FIGURE 1.1: Graphic Organizer for Brainstorming

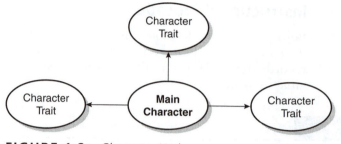

FIGURE 1.2: Character Web

3. Students trace both of their hands on the large paper. The same student partners or groups who worked together on the brainstorming activity and character web can complete the hand portraits.

4. The left hand will contain biographical information about the character. The teacher observes students to determine their mastery of content during this part of the activity.

5. The right hand will have character traits on each finger. The students may use their character web as a reference tool if they have trouble recalling information.

6. The palm of each hand will have a symbol for the character that reflects his or her central trait. The pair or group must agree on the representation of that trait.

7. The students present their hand portraits to the class and support their choices of character traits with evidence from the text. As each pair or group presents, the teacher rates the presentation with the assessment checklist.

An Application of Character Hand Portraits for Grade 5

Ms. Prendergast's fifth-grade class has just completed their first book in a literature study of the *Harry Potter* series by J. K. Rowling. As one of the culminating activities, the students are completing Character Hand Portraits in heterogeneous groups. These portraits are based on the first book, *Harry Potter and the Sorcerer's Stone* (1998). The students discuss how their character webs changed from the first versions, when they stopped at the midpoint of the book, to when they finally finished reading the whole text. Jennifer's group comments that in the beginning, they thought Harry was lonely and afraid, but their opinion changed when he entered Hogwarts School. The students remark that as a student, Harry earned a lot of points for the Gryffindor House because of his brave deeds. The Character Hand Portrait completed by Jennifer's group is illustrated in Figure 1.3.

Assessment Procedure

The purpose of the Annotated Checklist for Story Comprehension (Figure 1.4) is to guide the teacher in analyzing students' analyses of the main character in a story. When students are completing an author study or literature unit, the teacher may want to note how the students' Character Hand Portraits become more elaborate as they develop a knowledge base about literary elements.

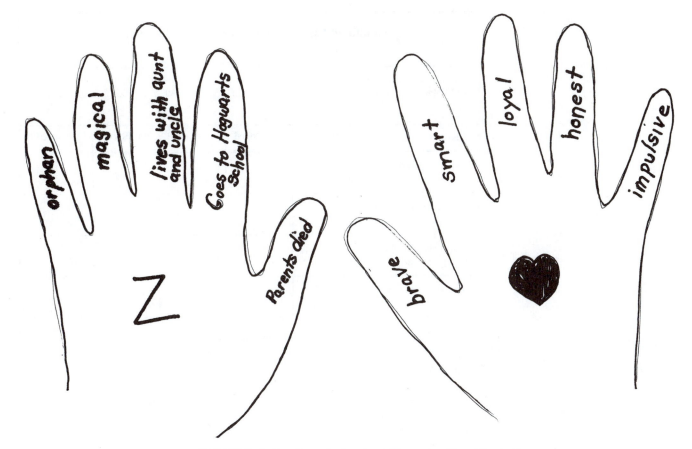

FIGURE 1.3: Sample Student Character Hand Portrait

Step by Step

1. As the students present their Character Hand Portraits, the teacher observes their performance and rates it according to the criteria in the checklist (Figure 1.4). The teacher may use the form as a template and modify it to suit specific instructional needs.

2. In order to extend the assessment procedure, the teacher can give the checklist to the students for self-assessment before they present their drawings. When students are given this opportunity, they should be allowed to make the necessary revisions to their presentations.

3. Teachers in the intermediate grades or middle school may distribute the checklist to the students for peer assessment. When students have an active-listening task to complete during discussion, it is easier for them to focus on the lesson.

Professional Resources to Explore

Carol Hurst Literature Website
www.carolhurst.com
This website provides teachers with titles of current award-winning literature as well as classic stories. It also provides lesson ideas to explore as well as author study units.

Annotated Checklist for Story Comprehension

Name _____   Date _____

Title of Book _____   Author _____

Benchmark	Beginning	Developed	Competent	Proficient	Advanced
Student identifies character traits.					
Student uses text to support traits.					
Student chooses symbol to represent character.					
Student presents portrait to class and supports choices.					

Comments

FIGURE 1.4: Annotated Checklist for Story Comprehension

International Reading Association
www.reading.org
This website provides teachers with current reports and articles on reading instruction as well as new literature titles for instruction.

Beach, R. (1993). *Reader response theories.* Urbana, IL: National Council of Teachers of English.

Daniels, H. (2002). *Literature circles: Voice and choice in book clubs and reading groups* (2nd ed.). Portland, ME: Stenhouse.

Keene, E. O., & Zimmermann, S. (1993). *Mosaic of thought: Teaching comprehension in a readers' workshop.* Portsmouth, NH: Heinemann.

References

Galda, L., & Cullinan, B. (2002). *Literature and the child* (5th ed.). Belmont, CA: Wadsworth.

Purcell-Gates, V., McIntyre, E., & Freppon, P. (1995). Learning written storybook language in school. A comparison of low SES children in skills-based and whole language classrooms. *American Educational Research Journal, 32*(3), 659–685.

Reutzel, D., & Cooter, R. (1990). Whole language: Comparative effects on first grade reading achievement. *Journal of Educational Research, 83*(5), 252–257.

Reutzel, D., Oda, L., & Moore, B. (1989). Developing print awareness: The effect of three instructional approaches on kindergartners' print awareness, reading readiness, and word reading. *Journal of Reading Behavior, 21*(3), 197–217.

Rosenblatt, L. (1978). *The reader, the text, the poem: The transactional theory of the literary work.* Carbondale: Southern Illinois University Press.

Children's Literature

Rowling, J. K. (1998). *Harry Potter and the sorcerer's stone.* New York: Scholastic.

A Strategy for Comparing Story Elements

INSTRUCTIONAL CONTEXT				
Grade Level	*Literacy Level*	*Group Size*	*Literature Genre*	*Literacy Skills*
● K–1	● Emergent	● Whole class	● Fiction	❖ Comprehension
● 2–4	● Early	● 8–10 students	○ Nonfiction	● Vocabulary
● 5–6	● Transitional	● 4–6 students		● Discussion
● 7–8	● Fluent	● Individual		○ Writing
				● Critical thinking

● *Applicable*	○ *Not applicable*	❖ *Target skill*

Framework for Instruction

The Literature Charts strategy provides a way to organize instruction around literature units. As children read, they take notes on each book related to the story elements and record their notes on a literature chart. One major benefit of using literature charts is that they serve as a resource for students when recalling elements from one book to compare with those of another.

A *literature chart* is a matrix drawn on a large sheet of chart paper and placed in the classroom where it will be visible to all students. Written along the top of the chart within separate boxes are labels of information related to the literature—for example, the title, the author and illustrator, and story elements related to the literature unit. The information for each book is recorded on each row of the literature chart.

The design of each chart is determined by the purpose for which the teacher will use it and the instructional context established for a particular class. For example, in a kindergarten class, a teacher is using a literature chart with children during an author study on Eric Carle and recording the children's personal responses to the character's problem in each book. In a third-grade classroom, students are reading versions of "Cinderella" and comparing the various story elements. Eighth-grade students from three different classrooms have developed an online literature chart. They are interactively analyzing the characters from three Gary Paulsen novels. In all of these cases, "book talk" plays a major role in responding to literature and developing the literature chart.

As teachers use more literature-based practices in their classrooms to support their literacy programs, issues related to management and organization often arise (Strickland, 1992). Literature charts, like language charts, have many functions: "A language chart in a classroom signals that children there read, talk about, and value books" (Roser & Hoffman 1995, p. 83).

Learner Outcomes

- The students will identify the story elements from books within a similar genre.
- The students will compare the story elements from a variety of books.
- The students will refer to literature charts as a resource in studying literature types.

Instructional Procedure

The design of each literature chart is determined by how it will be used. Literature charts have been used successfully in discussing stories, and they remain displayed in the classroom so that all students can refer to them when needed. When the charts are used interactively by students, they should be within students' reach. For example, if a group of students is working on one literature chart, it should be placed on the wall where the students are working and within reach so they can write on it.

Step by Step

1. The teacher prepares the students for the literature or author study unit. One approach is to give a brief "book talk" on each of the stories that will be included in the unit, emphasizing similar and contrasting elements across the stories.

2. The teacher sets up the general matrix for the chart on a large sheet of chart paper, making it visible to all students. The categories are determined by the literature that will be read.

3. Using the blank chart, the teacher and students work together to design the literature chart. When students are involved in setting up the chart, they will know how to use it. Literature charts are designed for specific literature units, reflecting the kinds of information that will be studied. For example, a literature chart on folktales will differ from one for an author study.

4. The teacher may give the students copies of the literature chart, depending on the ages and literacy levels of the students. When students have personal literature charts, the teacher directs them to use their charts during reading by taking notes to prepare for a discussion of the story. For younger students in kindergarten and first grade, the teacher should write the information on a large literature chart.

5. After reading the story, students participate in a discussion about the elements on the literature chart. The discussion includes the story elements, vocabulary words from the story, as well as personal responses and connections to the story that students make. When more than one story is read, comparing and contrasting the stories becomes an important part of the discussion.

6. The teacher and students fill in the information about each piece of literature discussed, as shown in Figure 1.5. Depending on the literacy levels of the students, the teacher may assume most of the responsibility for filling in the literature chart. For example, when students are at the emergent level of writing, they should dictate as the teacher writes. The responsibility may be left to the students when they understand the task and are fluent in reading and writing.

An Application of Literature Charts for Grade 3

In one third-grade classroom, the children have studied many versions of the fairy tale "Cinderella." The teacher began the study with a read-aloud of the traditional "Cinderella," by Charles Perrault (retold by Amy Ehrlich). After reading the story, the teacher and children discussed each element and added notes on the story to the literature chart. Each day, the teacher continued to read aloud another version of "Cinderella," followed by a discussion of the story. As notes on each new version of the "Cinderella" story were added to the chart, the

Title/Author	Characters	Setting	Magical Objects/Words	Initial Problem/Solution	Main Problem/Resolution	Reader Responses
Cinderella, by Charles Perrault	Cinderella, Fairy Godmother, Stepmother, and two daughters	Countryside	Fairy Godmother and her wand Carriage made from a pumpkin Horses transformed from white mice Glass slipper	Cinderella could not go to the ball like her stepsisters. Her Fairy Godmother performed magic and dressed her in the best gown. She also gave Cinderella a gilded coach to ride in with white horses to pull it.	At the stroke of midnight, Cinderella fled from the ball, leaving behind one of her glass slippers. When Cinderella was able to fit into the glass slipper, she was recognized as the princess and married the prince.	When one is kind, one is beautiful.
Yeh-Shen, by Ai-Ling Louie	Yeh-Shen, Stepmother, and her daughter, Fish	Southern China	Fish and fish bones Golden slippers	Yeh-Shen wanted to go to the spring festival, but her mean Stepmother would not allow it. Yeh-Shen got help from fish bones; he gave her new clothes.	Yeh-Shen ran away from the festival, so her stepmother would not see her, and lost her golden slipper. The king searched for the girl who had the golden slipper, and he found Yeh-Shen. They were married.	Kindness is rewarded with happiness, while wickedness is not.
Cinder-elly, by Frances Minters	Elly, mean sisters (Nelly and Sue), Godma, and Prince Charming	New York City	"Kerplike" Godma's cane Glass sneakers	Elly got tickets to go to the basketball game, but her sisters went instead. Her Godma waved her cane, and Elly got new clothes, glass sneakers, and a bike.	Elly hurried home, not to miss the 10 P.M. curfew, and lost her glass slipper. Prince Charming fit the glass slipper on Elly, and they lived happily ever after.	Elly forgave her sisters, and everyone learned a lesson of kindness.
Adelita, by Tomie de Paola	Adelita, Esperanza, Stepmother, and her daughter, Javier	Mexico	Rebozo—a shawl that belonged to Adelita	Adelita's Stepmother did not permit her to go to the fiesta. Esperanza came back, dressed her in her mother's rebozo, and Adelita went to the fiesta.	Adelita left the fiesta, afraid that Javier's family would forbid him to marry her. Upon searching for Adelita, Javier found her by recognizing the rebozo, and they were married.	To me, this was like another Cinderella.

FIGURE 1.5: Literature Chart for Different Versions of "Cinderella"

discussion took on the perspective of comparing story elements from the various fairy tales students had read and discussed. The children and teacher developed the literature chart shown in Figure 1.5 through students' responding to the teacher's questions and making personal connections and story responses.

Assessment Procedure

Students are expected to listen to the read-aloud and to engage in a discussion of the story. Students' responses and levels of participation will be the basis for assessing their story comprehension and discussion skills.

1. The teacher may focus on two or three students during the discussion and assess their levels of story comprehension. As students respond to the story elements, the teacher assesses their comprehension of the story using the assessment form in Figure 1.6.

2. The teacher observes other aspects of the discussion and documents various areas of literacy growth. For example, during the discussion, a student may use a vocabulary word from the story, demonstrate critical thinking, raise an interesting question about the story, offer a personal response, or show an exceptional interest in reading.

3. Another way to assess students' comprehension of a story is to have them complete their own literature charts. The teacher may wish to implement literature charts as an independent activity, in which students would complete the charts by themselves. In this case, the teacher would assess each student's completed literature chart.

4. The teacher uses the checklist shown in Figure 1.6 to document one student's responses during the discussion. The teacher checks the level of the student's response as determined by its quality:
   a. *Beginning:* The student is beginning to develop the target skill when he or she needs assistance to respond.
   b. *Developing:* The student is developing the target skill when his or her responses include the information that is mostly accurate.
   c. *Proficient:* The student is proficient in the target skill when his or her responses are complete and accurate.

Professional Resources to Explore

The Kids.Com
www.thekids.com
This site provides links to illustrated stories from around the world.

Bond, T. F. (2001). Giving them free rein: Connections in student-led book groups. *Reading Teacher, 54*(6), 574–584.

Hadaway, N. L., Vardell, S. M., & Young, T. A. (2002). *Literature based instruction with English language learners, K–12.* Boston: Allyn & Bacon.

Van Horn, L. (1997). The characters within us: Readers connect with characters to create meaning and understanding. *Journal of Adolescent and Adult Literacy, 40*(5), 341–347.

References

Roser, N. L., & Hoffman, J. V. (1995). Language charts: A record of story time talk. In N. L. Roser & M. G. Martinez (Eds.), *Book talk and beyond: Children and teachers responding to literature.* Newark, DE: International Reading Association.

Annotated Checklist for Assessing Use of Literature Charts

Name _____   Date _____

Literature Study _____   Grade _____

Literacy Behaviors	Beginning	Developing	Proficient
Identifies titles and authors.			
Identifies characters.			
Identifies settings.			
Identifies initial story events.			
Identifies story problem.			
Identifies story solution.			
Makes personal connections.			
Makes connections to other stories.			
Participates in story discussion.			

COMMENTS

FIGURE 1.6: Annotated Checklist for Assessing Use of Literature Charts

Strickland, D. S. (1992). Organizing a literature-based reading program. In B. E. Cullinan (Ed.), *Invitation to read: More children's literature in the reading program.* Newark, DE: International Reading Association.

Children's Literature References

Climo, S. (1993). *The Korean Cinderella.* New York: HarperCollins.
Climo, S. (1999). *The Persian Cinderella.* New York: HarperCollins.
de Paola, T. (2002). *Adelita: A Mexican Cinderella story.* New York: G. P. Putnam's Sons.

Hickox, R. (1998). *The golden sandal: A Middle Eastern Cinderella Story.* New York: Holiday House.

Johnston, T., & Warhola, J. (1998). *Bigfoot Cinderrrrrella.* New York: Penguin Putnam.

Louie, A.-L. (1982). *Yeh-Shen: A Cinderella story from China.* New York: Philomel.

Lowell, S. (2000). *Cindy Ellen: A wild western Cinderella.* New York: HarperCollins.

Minters, F. (1994). *Cinder-elly.* New York: Viking.

Perrault, C. (1985). *Cinderella* (retold by A. Ehrlich). New York: Dial.

Schroeder, A. (1997). *Smoky Mountain Rose: An Appalachian Cinderella.* New York: Dial.

Sierra, J. (2000). *The gift of the crocodile: A Cinderella story.* New York: Simon & Schuster.

Steptoe, J. (1987). *Mufaro's beautiful daughters: An African tale.* New York: Lothrop, Lee & Shepard.

Wilson, B. K. (1993). *Wishbones: A folk tale from China.* New York: Bradbury Press.

A Strategy for Developing Comprehension of Narrative Text

INSTRUCTIONAL CONTEXT				
Grade Level	**Literacy Level**	**Group Size**	**Literature Genre**	**Literacy Skills**
● K–1	● Emergent	● Whole class	● Fiction	❖ Comprehension
● 2–4	● Early	● 8–10 students	● Nonfiction	● Vocabulary
● 5–6	● Transitional	● 4–6 students		● Discussion
● 7–8	● Fluent	● Individual		○ Writing
				● Critical thinking

● Applicable	¡ Not applicable	❖ Target skill

A Framework for Instruction

In Oral Story Retelling, students retell a story orally in their own words after they have read or listened to it. While students retell the story to a group of peers, the teacher uses a prepared retelling guide to record what they remember from the story and to assist them with prompts and questions when they forget certain story parts.

Retelling a story was once considered the simple recall of facts after reading or listening to a story. However, story retelling involves more than remembering what one has heard or read. Retelling text is an effective assessment tool to monitor comprehension, and it plays a powerful role in the development of comprehension (Gambrell, Pfeiffer, & Wilson, 1985; Morrow, 1985). In fact, research suggests that when students retell stories, improvement is seen in their understanding of stories, in their development of concepts for a story, in the advancement of their critical thinking and problem solving, and in their oral language (Brown & Cambourne, 1987; Hu, 1995; Koskinen, Gambrell, Kapinus, & Heathington, 1988). A more current understanding of story retelling is elaborated in Bensen and Cummins's (2000) model, which highlights what children's story retellings can reveal: that is, what a child remembers, thinks is important to remember, and thinks he or she should retell; how a child does or does not organize and sequence information, makes inferences and connections, develops language from reading, and constructs meaning; and whether or not the child's organization matches that of the text (p. 6).

Children at any age or stage of literacy development can participate in the Oral Story Retelling strategy. One of the most appropriate means of introducing story retelling to young children is to use oral story retellings. The children listen to a story and retell it to a small group of children. For young children who are inexperienced in retelling a story, props such as puppets and flannel board cutouts should be used to assist them as they retell the story. For older students, engagement in oral story retellings fosters their oral language development and presentation skills. Students who listen often question the storyteller, and such questioning can evoke a lengthy discussion of the story, encouraging different points of view.

Learner Outcomes

- The students will retell orally a story they have read or heard.
- The students will include story elements in their oral retellings.

Instructional Procedure

Children who are at the emergent or early stage of literacy development and who are in the early primary grades may not have had experience with the Oral Story Retelling strategy. If that is the case, story props and illustrations can help in their initial stages of story retelling. After listening to or reading a story, students use felt board cutouts and the flannel board as they retell the story. Oral retellings also may be used with students in the elementary and middle grades after they have read the story. "Book language," or the vocabulary of the author, is more likely to show up in students' oral retellings.

Step by Step

1. The teacher selects a read-aloud that is interesting and age appropriate and that has a simple plot that students can follow. He or she then outlines the following:
   a. The main characters and the setting or settings
   b. The major problem and story events
   c. The story conclusion, including the story solution or resolution

2. For younger students, the teacher prepares props for them to use during their story retellings. Such props may include cutout figures of the main characters and the setting or major settings in the story or other appropriate puppets. The cutout figures and pictures of the settings and events may be mounted on oak tag to which a piece of felt has been attached to the back and then used with a flannel board. Another way to have students handle the props is to paste the paper figures on wooden Popsicle sticks. Other props, such as paper bag puppets and Beanie Babies, may be used to increase children's motivation to retell a story.

3. The teacher prepares students to listen to the story. Prior to reading the story to the students, introduce the book to the children by discussing the following:
   a. The title and author and the illustrations on the cover of the book
   b. The characters and the setting
   c. The initial event in the story that puts the story in motion and establishes the goal for the main character

4. The teacher reads the story with expression.

5. After the read-aloud, the teacher invites students to respond to the story ending and other story parts they may have found interesting.

6. The teacher then introduces students to the props for story retelling, asking them to identify each and to tell something about it.

7. The teacher invites one student to use the props in retelling the story. As the student retells the story, the teacher uses the retelling checklist to assess his or her story understanding. The other students are encouraged to listen attentively to the story retelling.

8. When a student does not remember a significant story part, he or she continues with the retelling to the end. After the child has finished the story retelling, the teacher uses the following questions to cue or help him or her remember:

   Character: Who was in the story? Who was the story about?

   Setting: Where did the story take place?

   Beginning of the story: What happened at the very beginning of the story?

   Middle of the story: What happened next? Then what happened? What did the character do next?

End of the story: How did the story end? Was the problem solved?

Response to the story: Did you like the story? Why or why not? What did you learn from the story? Why do you think the author wrote the story?

An Application of the Oral Story Retelling Strategy for Grade 1

Lydia Ross, a first-grade teacher, read the story *Babushka* by Patricia Polacco (1990) to the children. After the reading, the teacher brought out the felt board pictures of the story characters along with two pictures of the story setting. The teacher led the children in a brief discussion of the characters and the setting. She then asked one student to come to the flannel board to retell the story. Gary, the student, told the story using the felt board cutouts. As he proceeded through his oral story retelling of *Babushka*, Lydia assessed his retelling using the rubric shown in Figure 1.7.

Assessment Procedure

Step by Step

The teacher prepares the story retelling rubric before the student begins to retell the story.

1. The teacher listens carefully to the story retelling. As the student is engaged in the story retelling, the teacher marks each part that the student retells. For example, when the character is mentioned, the teacher places a checkmark (✓) next to the appropriate box.
    a. If the student talks about the character, elaborating on the personality traits with two or three sentences, place a checkmark in the column under "E" for "Elaborated."
    b. If the student retells the story with no elaborations, place a checkmark under "D" for "Developing."
    c. If the student retells the story without mentioning a story element, such as the character, use a cue question to prompt that story part. If the student remembers a story element only after receiving a prompt, place a checkmark next to the element under "C" for "Cued." However, if the student cannot remember the character, place a dash (–) in the column labeled "Cued."

2. The teacher continues marking the assessment form until the child has finished.

3. The teacher carefully listens to the language used in the story retelling. During the child's story retelling, listen to the student's language for any words that are from the book. Write the student's vocabulary words in the row marked "Book Language."

Professional Resources to Explore

Benson, V., & Cummins, C. (2000). *The power of retelling: Developmental steps for building comprehension.* Bothell, WA: Wright Group.

Morrow, L. M. (1985). Retelling stories: A strategy for improving young children's comprehension, concept of story structure, and oral language. *Elementary School Journal, 85*(5), 647–661.

References

Benson, V., & Cummins, C. (2000). *The power of retelling: Developmental steps for building comprehension.* Bothell, WA: Wright Group.

Rubric for Assessing Oral Story Retelling

Name _____   Date _____

Grade _____   Literacy Level: _____ Emergent   _____ Early   _____ Fluent

Title of Book _____

Story Elements	Cue Questions	E	D	C
Characters	Who was in the story? Who else was the story about?			
Setting	Where did the story take place?			
Events				
Beginning of the story	What happened at the beginning of the story?			
Problem	What was _____ problem? What happened then?			
Middle of the story	What did _____ do next?			
End of the story	How did the story end?			
Response to the Story	Tell why you enjoyed or disliked the story. How did you feel about the character?			
Book Language				

Legend for Scoring the Story Retelling Assessment Rubric

Developing:	The child briefly mentions any one of the elements or embeds it into another element; the child makes a very short personal response of three to five words.
Elaborated:	The child spends time discussing the element using two to three sentences.
Cued:	When the child does not remember a story element, the teacher asks an appropriate question to help the child retell that part.
Book Language:	Write the special words from the book that the child uses in his or her story retelling.

FIGURE 1.7: Rubric for Assessing a Beginner's Oral Story Retelling

Brown, H., & Cambourne, B. (1987). *Read and retell: A strategy for the whole-language/natural learning classroom.* Portsmouth, NH: Heinemann.

Gambrell, L. B, Pfeiffer, W., & Wilson, R. (1985). The effect of retelling upon reading comprehension and recall of text information. *Journal of Educational Research, 78,* 216–220.

Koskinen, P. S., Gambrell, L. B., Kapinus, B. A., & Heathington, B. S. (1988). Retelling: A strategy for enhancing students' reading comprehension. *Reading Teacher, 41*(9), 892–896.

Morrow, L. M. (1985). Reading and retelling stories: Strategies for emergent readers. *Reading Teacher, 41*(9), 892–896.

Children's Literature References

Polacco, P. (1990). *Babushka.* New York: Simon & Schuster.

STRATEGY 4 PLOT PROFILES

A Strategy for Teaching Plot Development and Relationships through Graphing Story Excitement

INSTRUCTIONAL CONTEXT				
Grade Level	*Literacy Level*	*Group Size*	*Literature Genre*	*Literacy Skills*
○ K–1	○ Emergent	● Whole class	● Fiction	❖ Comprehension
○ 2–4	○ Early	● 8–10 students	○ Nonfiction	● Vocabulary
● 5–6	● Transitional	● 4–6 students		● Discussion
● 7–8	● Fluent	● Individual		○ Writing
				● Critical thinking

● *Applicable*	○ *Not applicable*	❖ *Target skill*

A Framework for Instruction

The Plot Profile strategy, developed by Johnson and Louis (1987), facilitates students in their understanding of how the tension within a plot changes by tracking the "highs" and "lows," or excitement, within a story. After reading the story and identifying the most exciting parts, or the *story tension,* students use a scale of 0 through 10 to rate the levels of excitement for the important story elements and events. A high degree of excitement is rated as a 10, and a story part that has little or no excitement is rated as a 1 or a 0. Using a line graph, the story tension is plotted to show the rise and fall of excitement within the story. On the *x* axis, the story excitement is recorded, and on the *y* axis, the chapters or story events are recorded. An example of a line graph for tracking story tension is shown in Figure 1.8.

Readers can use the structure of the plot to assist them in understanding the story because the story's elements are constructed around its plot, helping

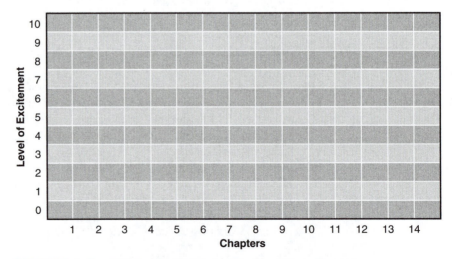

FIGURE 1.8: Plot Profile Graph for Tracking Story Tension

to achieve unity and coherence. Teachers typically use *story maps* and *story pyramids* that focus on the structure or organization of the story to support students as they develop their sense of story. The use of such strategies deepens students' understanding of a story by helping them to see its various parts.

However, students need to go further in understanding story organization and structure by examining the progression of story tension. Within a story, incidents and events cause action at various levels and lead to a resolution of dramatic tension. Thus, many stories are filled with "highs" and "lows" with respect to tension. Eeds and Peterson (1995) suggest that understanding the structure of the plot *tension* is more important than knowing the plot. They define the tension within the plot as "the suspense, anxiety, nervousness, strain, urgency, excitement, or fear that grips us as we read" (p. 13). Readers' experiences thus inform them when a story is filled with tension, and it prevents them from putting the story down.

Learner Outcomes

- The students will develop the concept of *story tension* and be able to identify the story parts in which it appears.
- The students will use the plot profile graph to represent the degree of excitement in the story generated by each story element.

Instructional Procedure

The Plot Profile strategy may be used with longer stories that contain chapters or with short picture story books. When applying the strategy to a chapter book, the students will rate each chapter for its tension or degree of excitement. For short picture story books, the most important story events are listed and numbered, and then each is rated for its degree of excitement. The Step by Step procedure that follows may be used to demonstrate to students how to use plot profiles to show the tension within a story. It will use a short picture story book. When students learn how to use plot profiles, they can work on independent activities.

Step by Step

1. The teacher reads the selected story to the students, or the students may read it independently.

2. The teacher conducts a discussion or a "grand conversation" with the students around the story elements. As they mention each story element, the teacher directs the students to list it on the chalkboard, and to number in correct sequence.

3. The teacher uses a prepared graph for the plot profile, similar to the one in Figure 1.8. A large sheet of graph paper fastened to the wall or chalkboard is suitable for using the plot profile graph with a group of students.

4. The teacher shows the students how to place the story elements along the horizontal (x) axis by using the number of the story element.

5. The teacher then uses the vertical (y) axis to demonstrate how to rate the degree of excitement attached to each element. To help students understand the concept of *tension* in a story, the teacher may ask them to tell the most

exciting events in their lives, rating them a 10. The teacher shows students where 10 appears on the graph, indicating a high degree of excitement. He or she requests them to think of other personal events and to rate them for excitement using a number from 0 to 10.

6. The teacher works with the students and guides them as they use the graph to plot the tension created by each story element. The students may decide to go back and change their ratings as their discussion about the story continues. In that case, they would be looking at the whole story and the relationships among the story elements by comparing tensions within the story.

7. When the graph is complete, the teacher directs the students to examine it for changing levels of tension within the story. His or her intention is to help students see the plot profile as a visual representation of the various degrees of tension and the relationships that story elements have in creating the tension.

8. When the students are ready to use plot profiles with longer stories, such as chapter books, the teacher assists them in plotting the excitement in each chapter. In this case, the students will examine the degree of excitement across chapters.

An Application of Plot Profiles for Grade 4

Michelle Walters used the Plot Profiles strategy to demonstrate how to graph the excitement in a story to her students in the fourth grade. She decided to use a read-aloud of *Lon Po Po*, by Ed Young (1996). This story is a Chinese version of "Little Red Riding Hood," and the plot is filled with varying degrees of excitement. After reading the story, Michelle conducted a "grand conversation" with a focus on the story elements and the tension within the story that was created by each event. As the students talked about each story element, Michelle asked them to write it on the chart. She guided them in numbering each element in the order in which it appeared. Michelle introduced the plot profile and told students how they could use it to graph degrees of excitement within the story. She guided the students in plotting the story elements and in graphing the tension each created in *Lon Po Po*. Figure 1.9 shows the plot profile of the story *Lon Po Po*.

Assessment Procedure

Assessment in the Plot Profile strategy involves determining whether the students understand the concept of *tension* within a story and how story elements differ in their degree of creating such tension. Students' proficiency in using the plot profile graph to visually represent story tension is assessed, as well.

Step by Step

1. After the students have completed their plot profiles, the teacher collects and evaluates them.

2. Using the form in Figure 1.10, the teacher assesses the students' performance related to their understanding of story tension by analyzing their graphs.

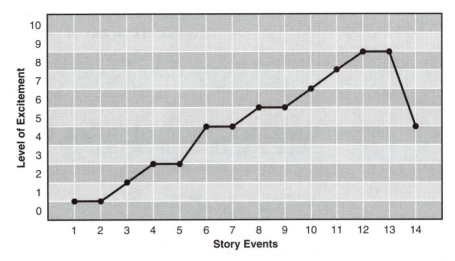

1. The three children were left alone by their mother so that she could visit their grandmother on her birthday.

2. This did not frighten the children.

3. A wolf in disguise tricked the children and made his way into the house.

4. The wolf was dressed like the children's grandmother and said that he was sick and wanted to come into the house.

5. The children let the wolf come into the house.

6. Shang, the eldest child, soon discovered that the wolf was not their Po Po when she felt its tail and its claws and saw its face in the candlelight.

7. Shang decided to trick Lon Po Po, "Granny Wolf," by tempting it with gingko nuts.

8. She told the wolf that they were sweet and delicious and magic.

9. Shang made up a plan and told her two sisters.

10. The three girls would climb to the top of the gingko tree and persuade the wolf to come up to eat the nuts.

11. They let down a basket for Lon Po Po to climb in and be lifted by them up to the top of the tree.

12. Each time they lifted the wolf a little higher, they dropped him to the bottom of the tree until he was lifted to the very top and dropped.

13. This allowed Shang, Tao, and Paotze to escape into their house.

14. They locked the door until their mother returned.

FIGURE 1.9: Plot Profile of *Lon Po Po*

3. The teacher uses the following categories to assess each student's graph:
    a. *Beginning:* The student needs assistance in identifying and sequencing story elements, attributing the tension created by story elements, and graphing different degrees of excitement within the story.
    b. *Developing:* The student is able to identify and sequence the story elements, to attribute the tension created by story elements, and to graph different degrees of excitement within the story with few errors.
    c. *Proficient:* The student is able to identify and sequence the story elements, to attribute the tension created by story elements, and to graph different degrees of excitement within the story with no errors.

4. During the "grand conversation" about the book, the teacher observes and documents student participation. Student discussions provide an excellent opportunity to assess comprehension. The teacher documents students' comments on the assessment form in Figure 1.10 under "Observational Comments."

Annotated Checklist for Using Plot Profiles

Student's Name _____   Date _____

Title of Story _____   Author _____

Literacy Behaviors	Beginning	Developing	Proficient
Identifies tension within story.			
Attributes appropriate degree of excitement to story events or chapter.			
Shows relationship between varying degrees of tension within story.			
Follows directions in plotting elements on graph.			

OBSERVATIONAL COMMENTS

FIGURE 1.10: Annotated Checklist for Using Plot Profiles

Professional Resources to Explore

Assessing with Rubrics
http://intranet.cps.k12.il.us/Assessments/Ideas_and_Rubrics/
ideas_and_rubrics.html
This website looks at using rubrics to assess student learning and provides sample rubrics.

Barton, J. (2001). *Teaching with children's literature.* Norwood, MA: Christopher-Gordon.

Hadaway, N. L., Vardell, S. M., & Young, T. A. (2002). *Literature based instruction for English language learners, K–12.* Boston: Allyn & Bacon.

References

Eeds, M., & Peterson, R. L. (1995). What teachers need to know about the literary craft. In N. L. Roser & M. G. Martinez (Eds.), *Book talk and beyond: Children and teachers respond to literature* (pp. 10–23). Newark, DE: International Reading Association.

Johnson, T. D., & Louis, D. R. (1987). *Literacy through literature.* Portsmouth, NH: Heinemann.

Children's Literature References

Young, E. (1996). *Lon Po Po: A Red-Riding Hood Story from China.* New York: Penguin Putnam.

A Strategy for Developing Comprehension of Text

INSTRUCTIONAL CONTEXT				
Grade Level	*Literacy Level*	*Group Size*	*Literature Genre*	*Literacy Skills*
○ K–2	○ Emergent	● Whole class	○ Fiction	❖ Comprehension
● 2–4	● Early	● 8–10 students	● Nonfiction	● Vocabulary
● 5–6	● Transitional	● 4–6 students		● Discussion
● 7–8	● Fluent	○ Individual		● Writing
				● Critical thinking

● *Applicable*	○ *Not applicable*	❖ *Target skill*

A Framework for Instruction

The Read to Discover strategy invites students to use focus questions to guide their reading of narrative or expository text. This versatile yet simple strategy uses focus questions to guide students through the comprehension of text. After the students have finished a passage, they write a summary of it.

The National Reading Panel (2000) defines *comprehension* as "an active process that requires an intentional thoughtful interaction between the reader and the text" (p. 13). In order to facilitate the active processing of text, the National Reading Panel urges teachers to use strategies that require students to connect their prior knowledge with new learning. The panel has concluded that comprehension occurs when readers engage in processes that require problem solving. When students construct knowledge by connecting prior knowledge with new concepts, they are actively processing text. After evaluating the research on comprehension instruction, the panel has concluded that seven instructional strategies are effective. The Read to Discover strategy incorporates two of these categories: question generation and summarization of text.

When students generate their own focus questions for reading, they are imitating the behaviors of effective readers. According to research, effective readers are aware of their purpose for reading and also read to find critical information (Pressley, 2000). Unfortunately, many of the students in today's classrooms are poor at comprehension. According to the RAND Reading Study Group (2002), teachers have reported that students need instruction that actively promotes the accessing of prior knowledge. Having prior knowledge, or *schemata,* is absolutely necessary for comprehension (Pressley, 2000). The comprehension of text depends on what the reader brings to the act of reading. If students are unfamiliar with the central theme or topic of the reading, the teacher must provide supplemental readings or assignments to build a mental framework. The Read to Discover strategy may be used to construct readers' schemata or to model the purposeful, critical reading of text (Unrau, 2004).

Learner Outcomes

- The students will generate a purpose for reading.
- The students will problem solve while addressing questions regarding the text.
- The students will summarize and respond to text passages.

Instructional Procedure

Step by Step

1. Students are assigned a text passage to read silently for homework or as a seatwork assignment. The teacher may want to pair any struggling readers heterogeneously for text reading.

2. At first, the teacher writes the questions for the passages. These questions can be generic, such as "Who was your favorite character?" or more specific, such as "Why did the Pilgrims leave England?" As the students become proficient in this process, they can work in pairs to generate questions for their own reading. Regardless, the questions are put into the "question basket" (see Figure 1.11).

3. Students pick questions from the basket. Students raise their hands when they find the answer in the passage and read it aloud for their peers.

4. After the questions have been answered, the students write a summary of what they have learned about the new topic or concept. The students must defend their summary with evidence from the text.

An Application of the Read to Discover Strategy for Grade 7

During the month of November, Mr. Hamilton's seventh-grade class began their study of colonial America with a unit on New England. The students began reading their textbook chapter on the Massachusetts Bay Company and settlement by the Pilgrims. Some of the students in the class had special needs and were not reading on grade level. In order to ensure that all students grasped the concepts of the unit, Mr. Hamilton placed the students into mixed-ability groups. James's group selected the question "Why did the Pilgrims leave England?" from the question basket. Mr. Hamilton assigned one student to do a read-aloud of the chapter for the group while the other group members took notes. After read-

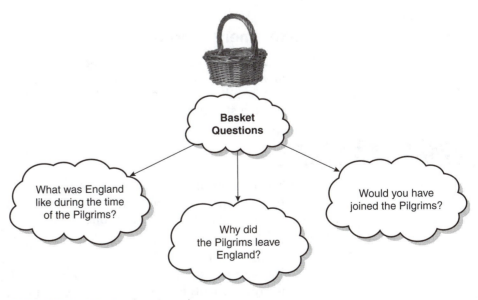

FIGURE 1.11: Basket Questions

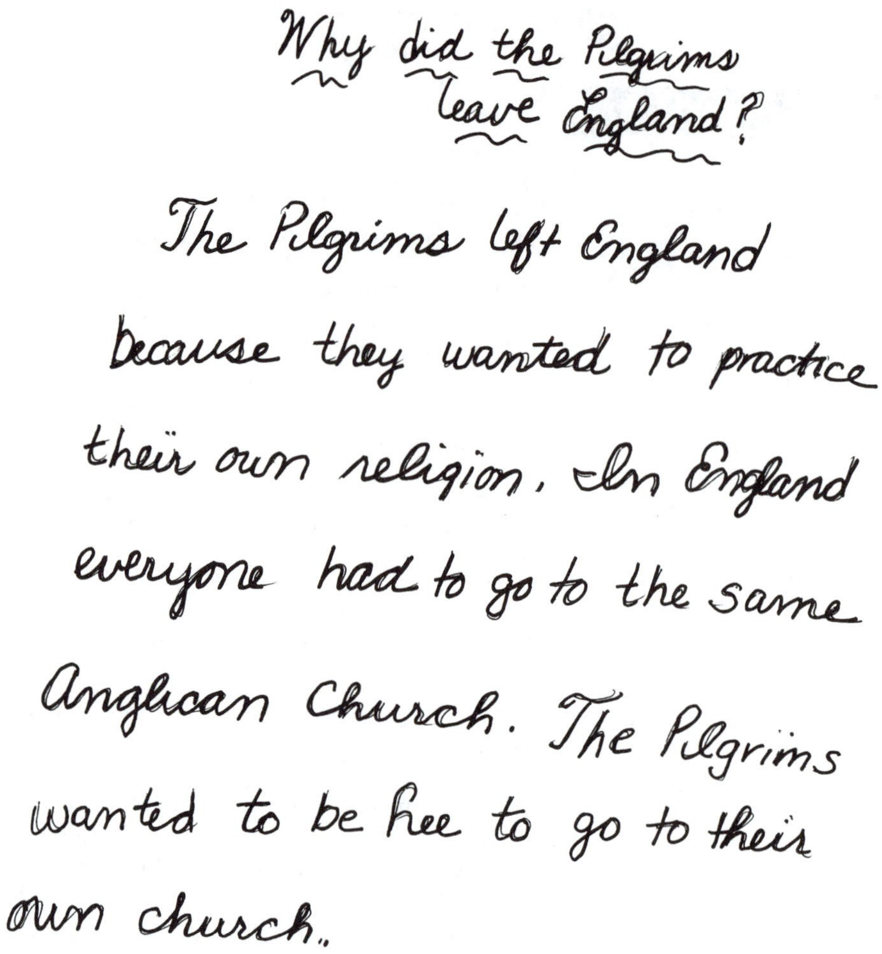

Why did the Pilgrims leave England?

The Pilgrims left England because they wanted to practice their own religion. In England everyone had to go to the same Anglican Church. The Pilgrims wanted to be free to go to their own church.

FIGURE 1.12: Sample Student Response

ing the chapter, James's group wrote the response shown in Figure 1.12 as an answer to their basket question.

Assessment Procedure

The purpose of the checklist for the Read to Discover strategy is to help the teacher analyze students' comprehension during focused reading. The checklist can be administered each grading period to provide a developmental profile of each student's progress.

Step by Step

1. The teacher observes students' performance throughout the activity using the checklist shown in Figure 1.13. If the teacher has a large class, it might be more practical to observe one group at a time.

2. As each student demonstrates the benchmark performance, the teacher writes an anecdotal comment or checks the appropriate box. The teacher should note if a particular area, such as generating questions, is difficult for the student. English language learners may struggle with content-area reading if they do not have prior knowledge about the topic.

Annotated Checklist for Read to Discover Strategy

Name _____   Grade _____

Observer _____   Text _____

	Beginning	Developed	Competent	Proficient
Student generates questions.				
Student skims passage for answers.				
Student writes summary of passage.				
Student participates in discussion.				
Student presents portrait to class and supports choices.				

COMMENTS

SUMMARY OF PERFORMANCE

FIGURE 1.13: Annotated Checklist for Read to Discover Strategy

Professional Resources to Explore

Read/Write/Think
www.readwritethink.org
This website is focused on integrating critical thinking and literacy.

Reading Online
www.readingonline.org
Teachers can access this site for myriad activities for literacy instruction.

Langer, E. (1997). *The power of mindful learning*. Reading, MA: Addison-Wesley.
Lieberman, M., & Langer, E. (1995). Mindfulness and the process of learning. In P. Antonacci (Ed.), *Learning and context*. Creskill, NJ: Hampton Press.

References

National Reading Panel. (2000). *Teaching children to read: An evidence-based assessment of the scientific research literature on reading and its implications for reading instruction.* Washington, DC: National Institute of Child Health and Human Development.

Pressley, M. (2000). What should comprehension instruction be the instruction of? In M. L. Kamil, P. B. Mosenthal, P. D. Pearson, & R. Barr (Eds.), *Handbook of Reading Research* (Vol. 3, pp. 545–563). White Plains, NY: Longman.

RAND Reading Study Group. (2002). *Reading for understanding: Toward an R&D program in reading comprehension.* Washington, DC: Office of Education Research and Improvement (OERI).

Unrau, N. (2004). *Content area reading and writing: Fostering literacies in middle and high school cultures.* Upper Saddle River, NJ: Pearson.

A Strategy That Encourages an Aesthetic Response to Literature

INSTRUCTIONAL CONTEXT				
Grade Level	*Literacy Level*	*Group Size*	*Literature Genre*	*Literacy Skills*
● K–1	● Emergent	● Whole class	● Fiction	❖ Comprehension
● 2–4	● Early	● 8–10 students	○ Nonfiction	○ Vocabulary
● 5–6	● Transitional	● 4–6 students		● Discussion
● 7–8	● Fluent	● Individual		● Writing
				● Critical thinking

● *Applicable*	○ *Not applicable*	❖ *Target skill*

A Framework for Instruction

The Sketch-to-Stretch strategy encourages students to respond to literature through the use of a different print media—drawing. Rather than discuss or write about the author's meaning, students are asked to think about what the story meant to them (Harste, Short, & Burke, 1988). Students then sketch their personal meanings and responses to the story as they utilize another resource for self-expression.

Such responses tend to be enhanced with new meanings. Gardner (1980) explains that children's drawings are filled with "interesting mixes of graphic and linguistic resources, in the service of complex conceptualization" (p. 154). The Sketch-to-Stretch strategy places an emphasis on the aesthetic response to reading, in which students are required to make personal interpretations of the selection they read. An *aesthetic response* is produced when "the reader's attention is centered directly on what he is living through during his relationship with the particular text" (Rosenblatt, 1978, p. 25). Using drawings to express his or her interpretation of the text allows the student to generate new meanings and go beyond the traditional verbal response to literature. Therefore, the teacher who uses this visual response strategy assumes that in constructing their responses to literature, readers bring their own personal experiences and emotions to the text, which will lead them to make unique interpretations of it.

Because the Sketch-to-Stretch strategy uses a visual interpretation of the story in the form of a drawing, it may be used with students in all grades and at all literacy levels. Students who are in kindergarten at the emergent literacy level and not fluent in writing will feel comfortable expressing their responses using sketches, and students at the intermediate and middle grades will use sketches to complement their written responses. English language learners who are not yet proficient in writing will be encouraged to offer richer interpretations of stories through their drawings.

Learner Outcomes

- The students will interpret the story through a combination of pictures and words.
- The students will go beyond the author's meaning using personal responses and interpretations.

Instructional Procedure

The purpose of the Sketch-to-Stretch strategy is to offer students the opportunity to respond to a piece of literature in unique ways based on how they feel while reading the story or how they interpret the text because of their own related experiences. Therefore, in preparing children for this strategy, it is important to emphasize the importance of making personal story interpretations and responses.

Step by Step

1. The teacher provides each student with the necessary materials: paper; pencils, crayons, or markers for sketching; and a copy of the book to be read.

2. The teacher prepares students for reading the story through a brief book introduction. During the book introduction, it is important to help students make personal connections to the story that will evoke a variety of aesthetic responses.

3. The students may work in small groups or individually. The teacher introduces the Sketch-to-Stretch strategy by encouraging students to draw their responses, interpretations, and feelings during and after their readings. At this point, the teacher encourages students to experiment with their interpretations and emphasizes that there are many ways to interpret a story. In explaining the purpose of *sketching* the meaning of the story, personal interpretations should be emphasized over the artistic quality of the drawings.

4. The teacher provides ample time for students to complete their sketches. After the students have sketched their responses, the teacher asks them to write explanations of their interpretations under their sketches.

5. The teacher encourages students to share their story interpretations and responses. In small groups or with the whole class, the students may share their sketches and responses to the story.

6. The sketches of the story may be displayed. One idea is to create a collage of the students' sketches, showing multiple interpretations of the same story.

An Application of Sketch-to-Stretch for Grade 3

The third-grade students in Karen's class were engaged in a variety of author studies. One literature circle was reading Eve Bunting's works. This group of eight students had just completed reading and discussing a book about a visit by a young boy and his father to the Vietnam War Memorial in Washington, DC, where they found the boy's grandfather's name. For a follow-up activity to the discussion, the teacher used the Sketch-to-Stretch strategy to encourage students' personal responses to the story. Figure 1.14 is one student's Sketch-to-Stretch response to the book *The Wall*.

Assessment Procedure

Students' comprehension of the story should be deeper because they are engaged in using multiple modes of communication—reading, drawing, writing, discussion, and sharing—to interpret the story. Therefore, the teacher should assess how the students use drawing to respond to the story, writing to summarize their responses, and discussion to share their story responses with others.

They look at the wall and read so many names of brave soldiers. They are dead and they are still with us because we remember them.

A Sketch to Stretch
The Wall
by
Eve Bunting

FIGURE 1.14: Sample Student Drawing

Step by Step

1. The teacher prepares for the assessment by completing a form for each student similar to the one in Figure 1.15.

2. The teacher observes each student sharing his or her Sketch-to-Stretch. Using the checklist in Figure 1.15, the teacher assesses the student's presentation skills.

3. The teacher then collects and assesses the individual sketches. Under the headings "Sketch-to-Stretch" and "Written Summary," the teacher assesses each student's work sample on the criteria related to the quality of both the drawn story response and the written interpretation.

4. The teacher uses the checklist to document students' responses during the discussion as well as their sketches and written personal interpretations.

5. The teacher marks the level of each student's response as described below:
   a. *Beginning:* The student needs assistance to make personal connections in his or her responses as well as to share those responses and to write accompanying summaries.
   b. *Developing:* The student's responses are based on some personal connections, and his or her presentation skills and written summaries are mostly accurate, containing only a few errors.
   c. *Proficient:* The student's responses are complete and show multiple personal connections to the story; his or her presentation skills and written responses are complete and accurate.
   d. *Advanced:* The student's responses demonstrate a complex way of thinking, as do his or her presentation skills and written summaries.

Checklist for Assessing a Reader's Response to Stories Using Sketch-to-Stretch

Name _____   Date _____

Book Title _____   Author _____

Literacy Behaviors	Beginning	Developing	Proficient	Advanced
Presentation/Sharing Response				
• Demonstrates understanding of story.				
• Demonstrates personal meaning of the response underlying illustration.				
• Demonstrates connection between story and personal response.				
• Makes presentation that is articulate, audible, and interesting.				
Sketch-to-Stretch				
• Illustrates thoughtful perspective of story response.				
• Illustrates personal connection to story.				
Written Summary				
• Sentence structure				
• Main idea				
• Supporting details				
• Conclusion				
• Spelling				
• Punctuation				
• Capital letters				
• Handwriting				

COMMENTS AND OBSERVATIONS

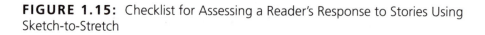

FIGURE 1.15: Checklist for Assessing a Reader's Response to Stories Using Sketch-to-Stretch

Professional Resources to Explore

Website for Picture Story Books
http://picturingbooks.org
This website offers rich information about picture story books.

Bussert-Webb, K. (2001). I won't tell you about myself, but I will draw my story. *Language Arts, 78*(6), 511–519.

Ernst, K. (1993). *Picturing learning.* Portsmouth, NH: Heinemann.

Whitin, P. E. (1996). *Sketching stories, stretching minds.* Portsmouth, NH: Heinemann.

References

Gardner, H. (1980). *Artful scribbles: The significance of children's drawings.* New York: Basic Books.

Harste, J. C., Short, K. G., & Burke, C. (1988). *Creating classrooms for authors: The reading-writing connection.* Portsmouth, NH: Heinemann.

Rosenblatt, L. (1978). *The reader, the text, the poem.* Carbondale, IL: Southern Illinois University Press.

Children's Literature References

Bunting, E. (1992). *The wall.* New York: Clarion.

A Strategy for Developing Comprehension of Narrative Text

INSTRUCTIONAL CONTEXT				
Grade Level	*Literacy Level*	*Group Size*	*Literature Genre*	*Literacy Skills*
● K–2	● Emergent	● Whole class	● Fiction	❖ Comprehension
● 2–4	● Early	● 8–10 students	○ Nonfiction	● Vocabulary
● 5–6	● Transitional	● 4–6 students		● Discussion
● 7–8	● Fluent	○ Individual		● Writing
				● Critical thinking

● *Applicable*	○ *Not applicable*	❖ *Target skill*

A Framework for Instruction

The Storyboard strategy is an excellent tool for facilitating students' responses to both narrative and expository text. Storyboards also enable students to develop schemata of narrative text and story grammar. In this strategy, students illustrate the main events in the story of one chapter of a book and present the storyboard to the class by retelling the passage.

Louise Rosenblatt (1978) developed the *reader response theory*, which stated that reading is a transaction between the reader and the text. Each reader develops his or her own interpretation of the text based on his or her life experiences and culture. Research indicates that as students improve their knowledge of narrative text structure, their comprehension improves (Fitzgerald & Spiegel, 1983).

Comprehension is an active process, as students use what they know to construct meaning from the text (Spivey, 1997). *Strategic readers* activate their prior knowledge in order to make connections with the text (Antonacci & O'Callaghan, 2004). When students lack prior knowledge, they may be unable to make connections or they may construct inaccurate concepts (Chinn & Brewer, 1993). Teachers who scaffold the comprehension process before, during, and after reading the text help their students to become engaged, strategic readers (Antonacci & O'Callaghan, 2004). The Storyboard strategy facilitates the comprehension of text as well as the development of schemata regarding narrative text structure.

Learner Outcomes

- The students will read a fictional story and use a story map organizer to take notes.
- The students will use their story maps to create storyboards.
- The students will retell the story using their storyboards and include story elements such as setting, characterization, and plot.

Instructional Procedure

The Storyboard strategy is an example of active literacy instruction, in which students process text before, during, and after reading. This strategy can be modified for students with special needs and for struggling readers.

Step by Step

1. Before students generate storyboards independently, the teacher models the process with photocopied illustrations from a picture book. The teacher only uses key illustrations to retell the story.

2. After the students read the story, they brainstorm the story elements on the story map in Figure 1.16. The students may use the text as a reference during brainstorming.

3. After the students have completed the story map, they can break into groups of three to create storyboards. Students must first plan the key events they will illustrate, and then they draw them on paper. The students' illustrations are glued to a poster board for presentation.

4. When the groups have finished their posters, they retell the story without using any notes. This retelling should be a performance, rather than a report. If the students need notes, they may use them, but they should gradually learn to retell the story from memory.

An Application of Storyboard Strategy for Grade 1

The first-grade class at Davis Elementary School had been studying Maurice Sendak as their first author study. Ms. Santiago paired the students and asked them to select their favorite Maurice Sendak story to illustrate in a storyboard. Diana and Lisa finished their story map of *Where the Wild Things Are* and then

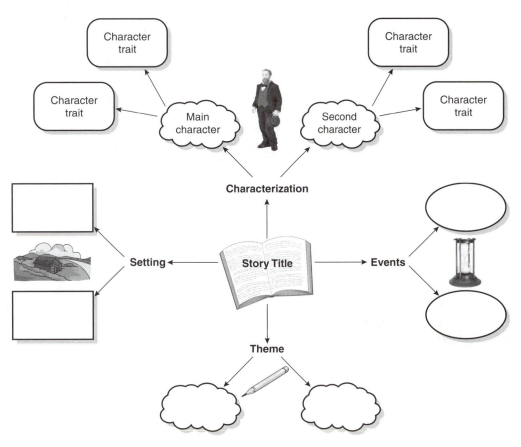

FIGURE 1.16: Story Map

FIGURE 1.17: Sample Student Storyboard

used it to focus on key events. Ms. Santiago facilitated the process by giving the students five panels to complete for their storyboards. Diana and Lisa used their graphic organizer to complete the storyboard as shown in Figure 1.17.

Assessment Procedure

The teacher uses the Annotated Rating Scale for Comprehension (see Figure 1.18) to guide him or her in analyzing each student's oral retelling of the story. A student's retelling of a story is an excellent indicator of his or her comprehension skills. A student that is able to sequence events and provide details demonstrates mastery of the comprehension process.

Step by Step

1. During the activity, the teacher observes the students' oral retellings of the story. The teacher can modify the form to observe a group of students or use it to focus on individual students.

2. If the student has to be prompted several times, the teacher would give the student a rating of 1. The teacher should note over the semester if a student continually has to be supported during oral retellings.

Annotated Rating Scale for Comprehension

Name _____   Date _____

Book Title _____   Author _____

Story Elements	1 ⟵——————⟶ 5 Beginning Proficient	Comments
Main Character Makes reference to main character with little or no description.		
Story Setting Describes setting in detail and with accuracy.		
Story Events Mentions one or two story events with no relation to problem solution.		
Story Presentation Retells story in dramatic fashion with expression and without notes.		

SUMMARY OF PERFORMANCE

FIGURE 1.18: Annotated Rating Scale for Comprehension

3. If the student is able to retell the story without any help, the teacher would give the student a rating of 5. The teacher should note if the student is consistently able to retell stories without help or only able to summarize simple story plots.

4. The assessment form should be used developmentally, so the instructor can see the student's progress over the course of the academic year.

Professional Resources to Explore

New Zealand Ministry of Education
www.minedu.govt.nz
The New Zealand government offers teachers a rich website with several activities that integrate literacy and oral language.

Speaking and Listening Skills to Preschool through Grade 3 Students
www.ncee.org
This site offers instructional strategies for oral language.

> Berko, G. (2001). *The development of language* (5th ed.). Boston: Allyn & Bacon.
> McCabe, A. (1996). *Chameleon readers: Teaching children to appreciate all kinds of good stories.* New York: McGraw-Hill.

References

Antonacci, P., & O'Callaghan, C. (2004). *Portraits of literacy development: Instruction and assessment in a well-balanced literacy program, K–3.* Upper Saddle River, NJ: Merrill.

Chinn, C. A., & Brewer, W. F. (1993). The role of anomalous data in knowledge acquisition: A theoretical framework and implications for science instruction. *Review of Educational Research, 63,* 1–49.

Fitzgerald, J., & Spiegel, D. L. (1983). Enhancing children's reading comprehension through instruction in narrative structure. *Journal of Reading Behavior, 15,* 1–7.

Rosenblatt, L. M. (1978). *The reader, the text, the poem: The transactional theory of the literary work.* Carbondale, IL: Southern Illinois University Press.

Spivey, N. N. (1997). *The constructivist metaphor.* New York: Ablex.

Children's Literature References

Sendak, M. (1963). *Where the wild things are.* New York: Harper & Row.

A Strategy for Teaching Story Elements

INSTRUCTIONAL CONTEXT				
Grade Level	Literacy Level	Group Size	Literature Genre	Literacy Skills
○ K–1	○ Emergent	● Whole class	● Fiction	❖ Comprehension
● 2–4	● Early	● 8–10 students	○ Nonfiction	● Vocabulary
● 5–6	● Transitional	● 4–6 students		● Discussion
● 7–8	● Fluent	● Individual		○ Writing
				● Critical thinking

● Applicable	○ Not applicable	❖ Target skill

A Framework for Instruction

The Story Mapping strategy uses a graphic organizer to guide students in their oral or written retelling of a story. As a visual representation of a generic story, the *story map* is used by students to help them recall the important elements of a story. It contains blank slots that represent the important parts of a narrative: the story setting, problem, elements, and resolution. A variety of graphic organizers can be used as story maps, covering a full range of complexity. Teachers choose one that is appropriate for the grade and literacy levels of their students and that matches the story that they will retell.

Students' understanding of text is affected by its *content* and its *structure*, or organization. For a narrative text, the structure is developed around the *plot*, which includes the characters and the setting as well as the problem, the story events, and the story resolution that make up the plot. In short, the plot is designed around the main character's problem and the events that lead up to a solution, or the story's resolution.

The Story Mapping strategy aids students in their development of story sense. It also facilitates students' recall of story parts in an organized way, as it offers a systematic and sequential means of ordering the story elements. Additionally, the visual structure of the map allows students to see the relations among the story parts. As a graphic organizer, the story map aids students as they visually reconstruct the parts of the story. Further, research suggests that the use of such graphic organizers enhances story comprehension for struggling readers and writers (Cunningham & Foster, 1978; Idol & Croll, 1985). This is especially true for students who have difficulty organizing ideas to retell a story they have read. In short, story maps are beneficial to teachers, providing the guided questions that students need to recall story elements.

Learner Outcomes

- The students will read a story and recall its elements.
- The students will use a story map to plot the story elements in sequence.

Instructional Procedure

The teacher will help students to comprehend a story by providing them with a strategy to recall the story in a systematic way. Using the Story Mapping strategy, the teacher introduces students to the story map by demonstrating how to use it to retell a story.

Step by Step

1. For younger students, the teacher selects a book that has a simple plot. For older students, he or she selects a book that has an explicit sequence of story events that is easy to follow. When teaching children how to map a story, it is best to use a piece of literature that has appeal and that has a straightforward plot.

2. The teacher introduces the story to the students. The students read the story or listen to the story as it is read to them by the teacher.

3. After students have read the story, the teacher provides each of them with a story map similar to one in Figure 1.19. Students should have their own copies so that they may work on them individually to map the story.

4. Using an overhead transparency or computer projection, the teacher reviews the story map by calling students' attention to each of its parts.

5. The teacher conducts a postreading discussion with the students, and they work together to map the story. When the students demonstrate that they are confident in using the story map, the teacher suggests that they complete their own maps individually.

6. For younger students, the teacher may model story mapping several times prior to having them work independently. In this case, after the students have heard or read a story, the teacher may conduct a discussion around the story elements. On a large sheet of chart paper, the teacher and the students work together to map the story. After several demonstrations of story mapping, the teacher may encourage the students to work in small groups or independently.

7. After the students have completed their story maps, they share them in small groups. There are several ways to share the story maps. Students may share their maps by retelling the story. A second way to share the story maps is to have children focus on one element, such as the characters or the theme, and conduct a "grand conversation."

An Application of Story Mapping for Grade 2

The students in Joel Mai's second-grade class finished reading and discussing the story *Mr. Lincoln's Way,* by Patricia Polacco (2001). In a guided discussion, Joel helped students to recall the various aspects of the story elements through questions related to the story parts. As the students responded to each question, Joel modeled how to record each response on the story map. The class worked together, discussing *Mr. Lincoln's Way* and filling in the parts of the story map shown in Figure 1.20. After Joel demonstrated to the students how to use a story map, they were able to map stories on their own.

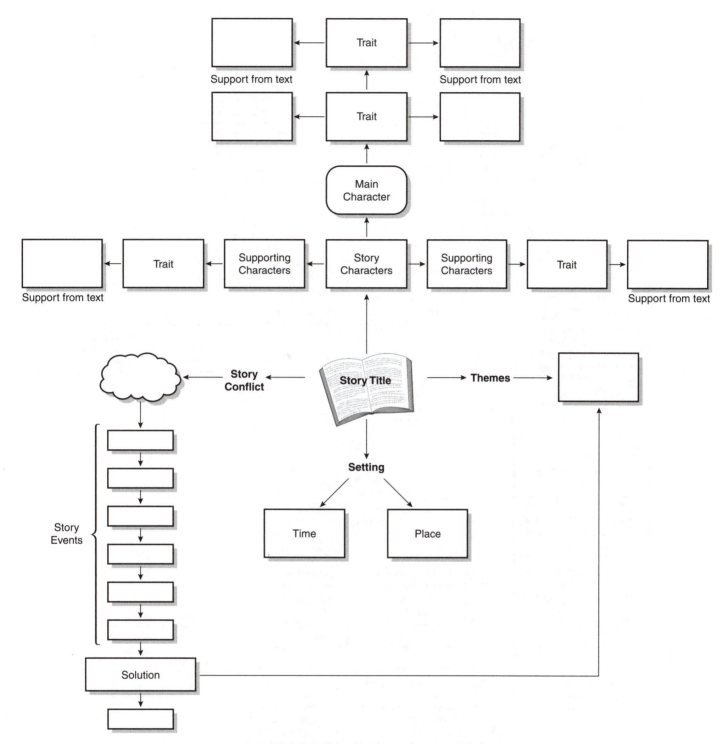

FIGURE 1.19: Sample Story Map

Assessment Procedure

When teachers use story mapping as an instructional activity, they will be interested in determining how much students recall from the story elements. Figure 1.21 may be used as a guide to assess readers at the early and fluent stages of literacy development as they present written story retellings.

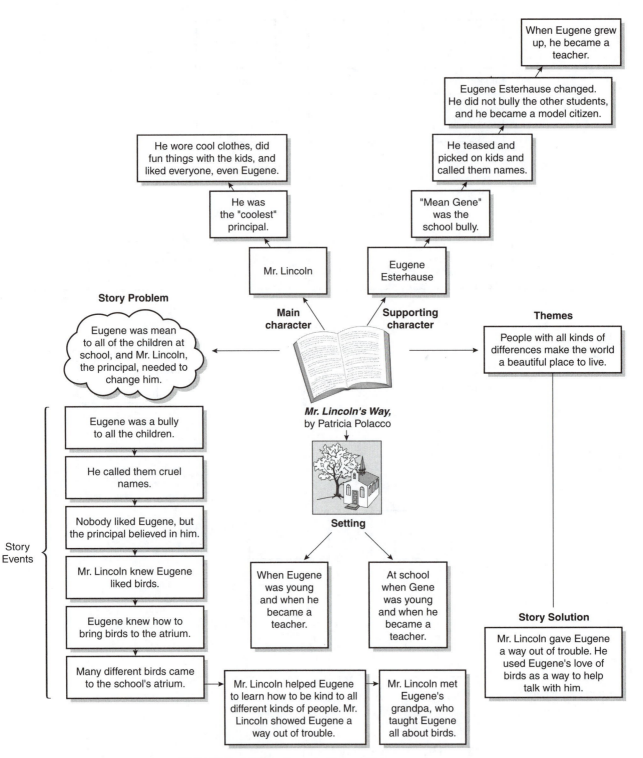

FIGURE 1.20: Sample Story Map

1. When the students have completed their story maps and shared them with the class, the teacher may use them to determine each student's comprehension of the story.

2. The teacher fills out the assessment form shown in Figure 1.21 for each student. The teacher uses the rubric to assess the student's level of recall of the

Rubric for Assessing the Retelling of a Story Using a Story Map

Student's Name _____ Date _____

Story Title _____

Story Elements	Cue Questions	E	M	C	N
			Check one box.		
Characters	Who was in the story? Who else was the story about?				
Setting	Where did the story take place?				
Events Beginning of the story Problem Middle of the story End of the story	 What happened at the beginning of the story? What was _____ problem? What happened then? What did _____ do next? How did the story end?				
Response to the story	Tell why you enjoyed or disliked the story. How did you feel about the character?				
"Book language"	Note the new and interesting words from the story that the student used in mapping the story.				

Legend for Scoring:

Elaborated (E): The student spends time discussing the element using two to three sentences.

Mentioned (M): The student briefly mentions one of the story elements or embeds it in another element and gives a short personal response of three to five words.

Cued (C): When the child does not remember a story element, the teacher asks an appropriate question to help him or her retell that part.

No Recall (N): The student does not recall the story element after the teacher gives a cue.

"Book Language": Write the special words from the book that the child uses in his or her story retelling.

FIGURE 1.21: Rubric for Assessing the Retelling of a Story Using a Story Map

story, the interesting words from the story that the student uses, and the student's response to the story.

3. The teacher assesses the student's story retelling using the following four levels of performance:
   a. *Elaborated:* This is the highest level of response. The student takes time discussing the story element using two to three sentences. He or she has a depth of understanding of the story element and is able to make connections.

b. *Mentioned:* The student briefly mentions the story element or embeds it in another element and makes a very short personal response of three to five words. The student has some understanding of the story element with limited recall.

c. *Cued:* When the student does not remember a story element, the teacher asks an appropriate question to help him or her recall it. The question is the cue that may facilitate the student's story recall. A cued response indicates a limited understanding of the story element.

d. *No Recall:* When the student does not remember a story element after the teacher provides a cue, he or she demonstrates a lack of recall for the story element or story comprehension.

English language learners and students at the emergent stage of literacy development may not include all of what they remember from the story in their written retellings because they are not fluent in writing. The teacher may ask these students to retell the story orally, using the rubric in Figure 1.21 to assess their understanding.

Professional Resources to Explore

Story Mapping Website
http://ocean.otr.usm.edu/~cboling/project/story.html
This website provides a discussion of using story maps, outlines the procedure, and offers a rubric for assessment.

Bromley, K. D. (1995). *Webbing with literature: Creating story maps with children's books.* Boston: Allyn & Bacon.

References

Cunningham, J. W., & Foster, E. O. (1978). The ivory tower connection: A case study. *Reading Teacher, 31,* 365–369.

Idol, L., & Croll, V. (1985). Story mapping training as a means of improving reading comprehension. *Learning Disability Quarterly, 10,* 214–229.

Children's Literature References

Polacco, P. (2001). *Mr. Lincoln's way.* New York: Philomel.

A Strategy for Developing Comprehension through Teaching Story Elements

INSTRUCTIONAL CONTEXT				
Grade Level	*Literacy Level*	*Group Size*	*Literature Genre*	*Literacy Skills*
○ K–1	○ Emergent	● Whole class	● Fiction	❖ Comprehension
● 2–4	○ Early	● 8–10 students	○ Nonfiction	● Vocabulary
● 5–6	● Transitional	● 4–6 students		● Discussion
● 7–8	● Fluent	● Individual		○ Writing
				● Critical thinking

● *Applicable*	○ *Not applicable*	❖ *Target skill*

A Framework for Instruction

The Story Pyramid strategy is designed to aid students in their development of story sense. This strategy is a structured approach that encourages students to think deeply about the character in the story along with other story elements. Students are asked to describe the parts of the story using a specific number of words. When they follow the directions, the students will construct a *story pyramid*.

Several factors affect reading comprehension. Among them is the structure of the text. For fiction, the structure of the text refers to the story elements, or *story schema*. Several early researchers (Kintsch, 1977; Mandler & Johnson, 1977; Stein & Glenn, 1979; Thorndyke, 1977) analyzed stories and found similar structures within narratives. When students have developed a schema for story—that is, when they have a familiarity with story structure—they experience greater remembrance and comprehension of stories. Using strategies such as the Story Pyramid will lead students to acquiring a more developed story schema or story sense.

Learner Outcomes

- The students will understand the parts of the story they have read or heard.
- The students will describe the story elements.
- The students will follow the directions to create a story pyramid.

Instructional Procedure

The instructional procedure is meant to encourage students to think deeply about the story they have read by applying their knowledge of story structure to it.

Step by Step

1. The teacher selects a piece of literature that has a clear and explicit plot. The story should be appealing to the students and at their level of understanding.

2. The teacher directs the students to read or listen to the story.

3. The teacher leads the students in a discussion of the story based on its elements. This discussion focuses on the main character, the time and place of the story, the story problem, the story events, and the resolution.

4. The teacher presents a blank copy of the story pyramid on an overhead transparency and provides blank copies to the students (see Figure 1.22). The teacher demonstrates to the students how to follow the directions to create the pyramid. For example, he or she reads the directions for completing item 1. Then he or she has the students work together in small groups on the story pyramid, assisting them when necessary. The teacher encourages the students to support their responses with evidence found in the text.

5. The students work through the story pyramid until they have completed it.

6. The teacher invites the students to share their story pyramids with the class. Consider different formats for sharing, such as creating larger groups from two small groups or whole-class sharing. Each group may work on a different piece of literature, and the sharing may be a way of introducing others to books that they may read later.

7. When students know how to follow the directions to complete the story pyramid, it may be used as a follow-up activity, with students working independently.

The Story Pyramid strategy may be modified when teaching the parts of speech to ask for adjectives, verbs, nouns, and adverbs instead of words to describe. For example, the following shows how items 1, 2, and 3 from Figure 1.22 were modified to use parts of speech:

1. Write one *proper noun* to name the main character.

2. Write two *verbs* to tell about the actions of the main character.

3. Write three *adjectives* to describe the setting.

Additional parts of speech may be used, depending on the background of the students.

This strategy may also be simplified for students who have special learning needs or find it difficult to follow a long set of directions. For example, an adaptation of the story pyramid may include three or four steps, rather than nine.

An Application of Story Pyramids for Grade 5

A small group of fifth-grade students in a literature circle was reading the book *Pictures by Hollis Woods*, by Patricia Reilly Giff (2002). After writing personal responses in their journals, the students engaged in a discussion about the story. At the conclusion of the discussion, the students completed a follow-up activity using story pyramids to summarize the book. Figure 1.23 is a sample of Joy's story pyramid of *Pictures by Hollis Woods*.

Assessment Procedure

When students have completed their story pyramids, the teacher may use their work to assess their understanding of the story as well as the depth of their personal responses. The assessment of students' written work will determine whether they can identify the story elements, make personal responses, and follow directions. Figure 1.24 can be used to assess an individual student's work sample. When students work in small groups, the form can be modified to assess the group's work sample.

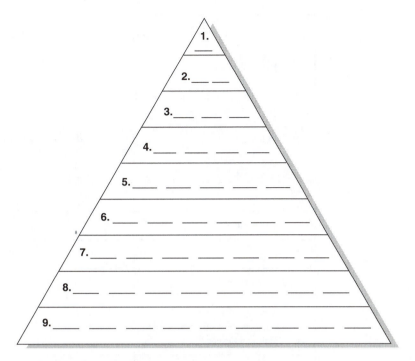

1. Name the main character.
2. Write two words describing the main character.
3. Write three words describing the setting.
4. Write four words stating the story problem.
5. Write five words describing the first story event.
6. Write six words describing the middle story event.
7. Write seven words describing the final story event.
8. Write eight words describing the solution/resolution of the story problem.
9. Write nine words describing a personal response to the story ending.

FIGURE 1.22: Story Pyramid Template

1. Hollis Woods
2. abandoned artist
3. many foster homes
4. runaway searching for family
5. loved Regan family but ran
6. with Josie forgetful old loving artist
7. Hollis and Josie run from Social Services
8. Josie returns to Beatrice Hollis returns to Regans
9. Hollis realized where there is love there's a Family

FIGURE 1.23: Sample Story Pyramid

Assessment Form for Story Pyramids

Name _____ Grade _____ Level _____

Title of Book _____

Story Elements	Degree of Accuracy in Describing Story Elements		
	Level 1	**Level 2**	**Level 3**
1 Main character			
2 Main character	,		
3 Setting			
4 Story problem			
5 Beginning story event			
6 Middle story event			
7 Final story event			
8 Story solution			
9 Personal response			

OBSERVATIONS AND COMMENTS

Level 1: Low degree of accuracy
Level 2: Average degree of accuracy
Level 3: High degree of accuracy

FIGURE 1.24: Assessment Form for Story Pyramids

Step by Step

1. The teacher prepares an assessment form for each student.

2. The teacher analyzes each student's story pyramid by determining his or her level of responses. For each story element, numbered 1 through 9, assess the level of performance:

   a. *Level 1:* Low degree of accuracy. The student's responses contain more than 50 percent of errors.

    b. *Level 2:* Average degree of accuracy. The student's responses contain some errors but less than 50 percent.

    c. *Level 3:* High degree of accuracy. The student's responses contain no errors.

3. After the responses have been assessed, the teacher may analyze the overall performance of the student to determine if there is a pattern of errors or areas that need further improvement.

Professional Resources to Explore

Multicultural Children's Literature
www.ncrel.org/sdrs/issues/educatrs/presrvce/pe_31k28.htm
The website offers listings and reviews of multicultural children's literature.

    Cunningham, J. W., & Foster, E. O. (1978). The ivory tower connection: A case study. *Reading Teacher, 31,* 365–369.

    Idol, L., & Croll, V. (1985). Story mapping training as a means of improving reading comprehension. *Learning Disability Quarterly, 10,* 214–229.

References

Kintsch, W. (1977). On comprehending stories. In M. Just and P. Carpenter (Eds.), *Cognitive processes in comprehension.* Hillsdale, NJ: Erlbaum.

Mandler, J. M., & Johnson, N. S. (1977). Remembrance of things parsed: Story structure and recall. *Cognitive Psychology, 9,* 111–151.

Stein, N. L., & Glenn, C. G. (1979). An analysis of story comprehension in elementary school children. In R. O. Freedle (Ed.), *New directions in discourse processing.* Norwood, NJ: Ablex.

Thorndyke, P. (1977). Cognitive structures in comprehension and memory of narrative discourse. *Cognitive Psychology, 9,* 77–110.

Children's Literature References

Reilly, P. G. (2002). *Pictures by Hollis Woods.* New York: Dell Yearling.

A Strategy for Developing Reading Fluency

INSTRUCTIONAL CONTEXT				
Grade Level	*Literacy Level*	*Group Size*	*Literature Genre*	*Literacy Skills*
○ K–1	○ Emergent	● Whole class	● Fiction	❖ Comprehension
● 2–4	● Early	● 8–10 students	● Nonfiction	● Vocabulary
● 5–6	● Transitional	● 4–6 students		● Discussion
● 7–8	● Fluent	● Individual		○ Writing
				● Critical thinking

● Applicable	○ Not applicable	❖ Target skill

A Framework for Instruction

The Weekly Reading Log strategy is an adaptation of using students' journal entries to record their responses and reactions to reading. It is used as part of the independent block of reading time that the teacher sets aside each day for students to read self-selected books. Students keep daily logs of their reading by recording the books they have read, the number of pages, and the time along with interesting words and short responses. The teacher expects students to assume responsibility for selecting books to read during the given time and for documenting what they have read by keeping a record, or *reading log.* Using weekly logs provides a way for the teacher and students to keep track of the amount of independent reading completed during the week.

There are many different types of reading logs, and each type is related to the specific purpose for the reading context. Tompkins (2003) describes students' reading logs as journals that they use to respond to their reading. That is, students write their opinions about or responses to the books they read in literature circles or book clubs. Journal entries can take many forms. They may include pictures about stories or written responses, or they may include focused questions that students pose about certain parts of a story. Some journals are used by students to summarize their daily reading, and other journals are kept by students who read about ideas they would like to include in their own writing. The teacher may use any combination of these by adapting weekly journal logs to fit the instructional context and student needs.

Students need time in school to read books that they have selected. Compelling research supports the positive effects that independent reading has on students' achievement in various areas of content learning (Anderson, Fielding, & Willson, 1988). Independent reading also provides students with opportunities to practice the strategies they have learned during formal reading instruction and to develop a positive disposition toward reading.

To promote independence in reading, teachers must commit to setting aside time during the day for independent or free reading (Routmann, 2000). The following are suggested guidelines for the effective implementation of independent reading:

- To develop reading routines for young children, be consistent with the time.
- Help children select material of interest at their own independent reading levels.
- Engage in "book talks" to stimulate children's interest.

- Highlight books by displaying them on open bookshelves.
- Make children accountable for the time they spend in independent reading.
- Have a class sharing time (Antonacci & O'Callaghan, 2004, pp. 248–249).

Learner Outcomes

- The students will select appropriate books for independent reading.
- The students will engage in reading during the time designated for independent reading.
- The students will keep weekly reading logs to include the number of pages they read as well as vocabulary words and short responses to their reading.

Instructional Procedure

The type of reading log that the teacher selects to use with students will be determined by his or her purpose and desired learner outcomes. This strategy uses the weekly reading log with the purpose of encouraging students to be accountable for their reading by monitoring how they use independent reading time. At the end of independent reading, each student marks the pages he or she has read, jots down any vocabulary words he or she has discovered, and writes a short response to his or her reading.

Step by Step

1. The teacher discusses with the students the purpose of the weekly reading log and demonstrates how they will record their entries. For all students, older and younger, the teacher may wish to model use of the logs.

2. The teacher distributes weekly reading logs to the students (see Figure 1.25). He or she shows students how to fill out the log for each reading session, writing the title of the book, marking the time spent reading, recording the pages read, and so on.

3. The teacher may demonstrate how to identify words that are interesting, challenging, or exciting. Sticky notes can be used to keep track of words during reading, and the words can then be recorded later.

4. The teacher discusses how to write a short response on the log. Responses should be short and express authentic reactions to the book. The teacher may select a day for students to share their readings and responses with others.

An Application of Reading Logs for Grade 4

Maura Campbell, a fourth-grade teacher, has established a routine for independent reading. Each morning, she sets aside a block of 20 minutes for silent reading by all students. They are required to be prepared by having self-selected library books to read. Maura knows that when students are prepared and have a high-interest book that they can read, they will spend the entire block of time reading. While the students read, they use sticky notes to flag new vocabulary words. After the allotted reading time, each student records the title of the book, the page numbers read, the new words learned, and a one-sentence response.

Assessment Procedure

When teachers provide blocks of time for independent reading, they expect students to use it wisely by engaging in reading their self-selected books for pleasure and for learning. Students may be encouraged to become accountable for the time they spend reading by making weekly self-assessments of their independent reading. Their self-assessment forms (see Figure 1.26) and their reading logs may be used by the teacher to assess how they are using independent reading time. The teacher may use both forms during a reading conference to discuss the time students spend on reading.

Step by Step

1. The teacher distributes self-assessment forms to the students at the end of the week. He or she conducts a brief discussion on the importance of self-assessment and answers any questions related to each item on the form.

2. The teacher reads each item with the students and asks for their interpretations. The teacher may give an example of an "Unsatisfactory" rating for each item and an example of an "Excellent" rating.

3. The teacher assists students as they assess their own independent reading performance for the first time. Depending on the maturity of the students, the teacher may work through the self-assessment form with the students item by item.

4. The teacher collects the reading logs and self-assessment forms weekly. The teacher may see a relationship between his or her observations of students' independent reading performances and students' self-assessments of their performances. The results may be used to help students use independent reading time more effectively.

MY WEEKLY READING LOG

Name _____   Week of _____

Day & Time	Title & Pages Read	New & Interesting Words Read	Short Response to Today's Reading
MONDAY Minutes _____			
TUESDAY Minutes _____			
WEDNESDAY Minutes _____			
THURSDAY Minutes _____			
FRIDAY Minutes _____			

FIGURE 1.25: Weekly Reading Log

SELF-ASSESSMENT OF INDEPENDENT READING

Name _____   Week of _____

Think of how you used the time during independent reading. For each item, rate your performance using a scale of 1 to 5.

How did I read this week?	1 ———————— 5 Unsatisfactory Excellent				
I selected a book that I could read and understand.	1	2	3	4	5
I read during the entire block of time, thinking about the story.	1	2	3	4	5
When I came to a part that was difficult to understand, I tried to make sense of it.	1	2	3	4	5
I thought about the words and wrote down those that I did not know or that were interesting.	1	2	3	4	5
I wrote honest responses to my readings.	1	2	3	4	5

FIGURE 1.26: Form for Self-Assessment of Independent Reading

Professional Readings

Predictable Books Website
http://monroe.lib.in.us/childrens/predict.html
This site provides a number of predictable books that will support younger children in starting to read independently.

> International Reading Association. (2000). *Providing books and other print materials for classroom and school libraries: A position statement.* Newark, DE: Author.
> Kuder, S. J., & Hasit, C. (2002). *Enhancing literacy for all students.* Upper Saddle River, NJ: Merrill/Prentice Hall.

References

Anderson, R. C., Fielding, L. G., & Wilson, P. T. (1988). Growth in reading and how children spend their time out of school. *Reading Research Quarterly, 23,* 285–303.

Antonacci, P. A., & O'Callaghan, C. M. (2004). *Portraits of literacy development: Instruction and assessment in a well-balanced literacy program, K–3.* Upper Saddle River, NJ: Merrill/Prentice Hall.

Routman, R. (2000). *Conversations: Strategies for teaching, learning, and assessing.* Portsmouth, NH: Heinemann.

Tompkins, G. E. (2003). *Literacy for the twenty-first century* (3rd ed.). Upper Saddle River, NJ: Merrill/Prentice Hall.

Instructional and Assessment Strategies for Developing VOCABULARY

Within this section are strategies to help students develop their word knowledge. Although the emphasis is on vocabulary development, students will be involved in using other forms of language to complete each activity.

A Strategy for Developing Vocabulary Skills

INSTRUCTIONAL CONTEXT				
Grade Level	*Literacy Level*	*Group Size*	*Literature Genre*	*Literacy Skills*
● K–2	● Emergent	● Whole class	● Fiction	● Comprehension
● 2–4	● Early	● 8–10 students	○ Nonfiction	❖ Vocabulary
● 5–6	● Transitional	● 4–6 students		● Discussion
○ 7–8	○ Fluent	○ Individual		● Writing
				● Critical thinking

● *Applicable*	○ *Not applicable*	❖ *Target skill*

A Framework for Instruction

The Interactive "Word Wall" strategy provides students with active learning experiences in exploring vocabulary. Students have multiple exposures to words through daily reading and writing activities as well as word study. "Word walls" also help struggling readers and writers by providing them with a ready reference for word patterns (Wagstaff, 1999).

Vocabulary acquisition is critical to reading improvement as well as writing skills. Research indicates that the best practice in vocabulary instruction tries to adapt strategies to fit the reading level of the child and his or her own individual needs (National Reading Panel, 2002). Effective vocabulary instruction also incorporates the following four principles:

- Students are active in learning new vocabulary.
- Personalized word learning is included.
- Students are immersed in words on a daily basis.
- Instruction builds on multiple sources of information for learning words through repeated exposures (Blachowicz & Fisher, 2000).

The following procedure describes how to implement Interactive "Word Walls" and to provide other formats of word study, which are described in the Application section.

Learner Outcomes

- The students will identify letter–sound relationships in words.
- The students will recognize word patterns.
- The students will use vocabulary words in reading and writing.

Instructional Procedure

Interactive "word walls" are implemented over the course of the week. The words are introduced on Monday, and during the week the students complete activities to explore word patterns. The number of words introduced each week depends on the age and level of the students. The following is meant as a general guide and may be modified for specific instructional needs:

Words Introduced per Week

Kindergarten: three words per week

First grade: five words per week

Second grade: five to eight words per week

Third and fourth grades: eight to ten words per week

The teacher chooses an appropriate literary selection to reflect the students' interests and reading levels. This procedure will describe how to use Eric Carle's *Walter the Baker* (1995) for an interactive literature "word wall."

Step by Step

The Interactive "Word Walls" strategy is easily adapted across grades and ability levels. It also helps English language learners to grasp new vocabulary.

Introducing the Words

1. The teacher begins by introducing the book and guiding the children through a "picture walk." The students make predictions, and the teacher records them on chart paper.

2. After the teacher has read aloud the story, the children join in the second reading as a shared book experience. English language learners may need more elaboration during the shared book experience. For example, the teacher might ask about their prior knowledge of certain words.

3. The teacher introduces the words on sentence strips, and the new vocabulary word is in a different color. The sentences provide a context for the new vocabulary word.

    baker: Walter the *Baker* was famous in his town.
    castle: The royal family lives in a *castle*.
    dough: The pretzel is made from *dough*.
    bakery: The *bakery* sells cakes and other sweets.
    pretzel: Walter created the first *pretzel*.

4. The teacher outlines the configuration of the word and asks the students to write the word in the air. The teacher prompts word study by asking the following questions:
    - What letter does the word begin with?
    - What sounds do you hear in the word?
    - Does it look like a word you already know?

5. When all the words have been studied, the teacher places them on the "word wall" according to categories, as shown in Figure 2.1. The teacher can model the process first, and as the students learn how to categorize words, they should complete this component.

6. The word cards should be color coded and cut according to word configuration to give the students help in identifying the words. For example, all *-ake* words can be coded red to help students recognize word patterns.

"Word Wall" Activities during the Week

1. *Magnetic letters:* Magnetic letters can be used to help the students actively learn the vocabulary words. Students can spell the words with the letters and then record the words in their journals or individual word books.

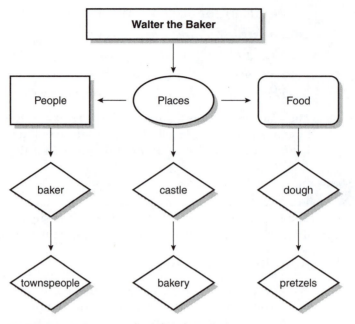

FIGURE 2.1: Sample "Word Wall"

Students with special needs may require magnetic letters with raised bumps to trace over the letters as they repeat the sounds.

2. *Pocket charts:* Pocket charts can be individualized or done with small groups. The students use letter cards to form the words and to blend the sounds.

3. *Illustrated word books:* Toward the end of the week, the students can create their own word books for *Walter the Baker* by illustrating each word and writing a sentence underneath the picture. If students prefer, they may write stories using the vocabulary words instead of disjointed sentences.

An Application of Interactive "Word Walls" for Grade 1

It is early December and Mr. Young's first-grade class is excitedly looking out the window at the first snowfall of the season. In response to such enthusiasm, Mr. Young decides to change his Interactive "Word Wall" activity by using the classic book *The Snowy Day*, by Ezra Jack Keats (1962). He gathers the students in the storybook corner and asks them to make predictions about the story before the read-aloud. After the students have joined in the second read-aloud through a shared book experience, Mr. Young presents the new vocabulary words on sentence strips:

snow: *Snow* falls during the winter.
crunch: I hear the snow *crunch* when I walk on it.
snowman: Peter made a smiling *snowman.*
piled: The snow was *piled* high.
pocket: My *pocket* has a hole in it.

After the students read the sentence strips, Mr. Young facilitates their awareness of the words by asking, "What do you notice about the words?" Andres responds, "I notice that *piled* and *pocket* both begin with *p!*" Mr. Young affirms Andres's answer and prompts the students further. "Do you notice anything else?" Jorgé raises his hand and excitedly blurts out, "I see that *snowman* has

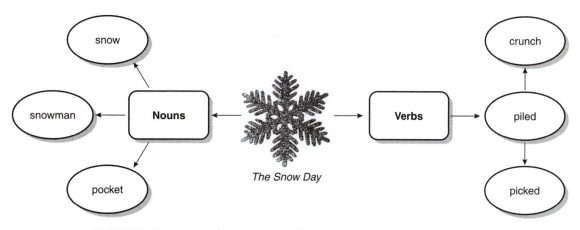

FIGURE 2.2: Sample Interactive "Word Wall"

snow in it!" Mr. Young congratulates Jorgé on pointing out the compound word and asks the students if they remember any other compound words from the story.

When all of the words have been discussed, Mr. Young directs the students to place the words in categories on the whiteboard. Since the students are studying the parts of speech, Marquis recommends that they be grouped as nouns, verbs, and adjectives. The students' categorization is illustrated in Figure 2.2.

Assessment Procedure

Interactive "word walls" provide the teacher with myriad opportunities to observe students' use of new vocabulary words in their reading and writing activities. The purpose of the Rubric for Assessing Vocabulary Acquisition, shown in Figure 2.3, is to guide the teacher in analyzing the students' vocabulary skills.

Step by Step

1. During the "word wall" activities, the teacher observes students' performances. For example, the teacher can observe how the students are using their prior knowledge to define new vocabulary words.

2. Based on his or her observations, the teacher rates each student's performance on benchmark skill behaviors by circling the appropriate box. The teacher should note if there are particular word families that a student is struggling with or if the student is unable to decode particular sounds.

3. For large classes, the teacher might want to focus on a fixed number of students each week. During the course of one month, every student in the class should be assessed.

Professional Resources to Explore

Learning Planet.com
www.learningplanet.com
This website offers teachers links and activities that focus on the development of decoding skills as well as word knowledge.

Rubric for Assessing Vocabulary Acquisition Using Interactive "Word Walls"

Name _____ Date _____

Grade _____ Topic _____

Vocabulary Skills	Beginning	Competent	Proficient
Letter–Sound Recognition	Student is unable to recognize letter–sound relationships.	Student is able to identify majority of letter–sound relationships.	Student identifies letter–sound relationships.
Word Patterns	Student is unable to compare new word with known word patterns.	Student is able to compare some words with known word patterns.	Student compares new word with known word patterns.
Definitions	Student gives erroneous definition.	Student gives partial definition and uses some context clues.	Student defines word and uses context clues from story.
Writing and Oral Speaking	Beginning	Competent	Proficient
Usage	Student does not use vocabulary words or gives incorrect usages.	Student uses some vocabulary words in writing.	Student uses vocabulary words in writing in proper context.

SUMMARY OF PERFORMANCE

FIGURE 2.3: Rubric for Assessing Vocabulary Acquisition Using Interactive "Word Walls"

Partnership for Reading
www.nifl.gov/partnershipforreading/publications/recommended.html
This website provides teachers with activities that are based on research evidence.

Buis, K. (2004). *Making words stick*. Portland, ME: Stenhouse.

Downer, M., & Gaskins, I. (1986). *Benchmark word identification/vocabulary development program*. Media, PA: Benchmark Press.

Snow, C., Burns, M., & Griffin, P. (Eds.). *Preventing reading difficulties in young children*. Washington, DC: National Academy Press.

Strickland, D. (1998). *Teaching phonics today*. Newark, DE: International Reading Association.

References

Blachowicz, C. L., & Fisher, P. (2000). Vocabulary instruction. In M. Kamil, P. B. Mosenthal, P. D. Pearson, & R. Barr (Eds.), *Handbook of reading research* (Vol. 3, pp. 503–525). Mahwah, NJ: Erlbaum.

National Reading Panel. (2002). *Report of the National Reading Panel: Teaching children to read.* Washington, DC: National Institute for Literacy.

Wagstaff, J. M. (1999). *Teaching reading and writing with word walls.* New York: Scholastic.

Children's Literature References

Carle, E. (1995). *Walter the baker.* New York: Simon & Schuster.

Keats, E. J. (1962). *The snowy day.* New York: Viking.

A Strategy for Developing Word-Solving Skills

INSTRUCTIONAL CONTEXT				
Grade Level	*Literacy Level*	*Group Size*	*Literature Genre*	*Literacy Skills*
● K–2	● Emergent	● Whole class	● Fiction	● Comprehension
● 2–4	● Early	● 8–10 students	○ Nonfiction	❖ Vocabulary
○ 5–6	○ Transitional	● 4–6 students		● Discussion
○ 7–8	○ Fluent	○ Individual		● Writing
				● Critical thinking

● *Applicable*	○ *Not applicable*	❖ *Target skill*

A Framework for Instruction

The Making Words strategy (Cunningham & Cunningham, 1992) focuses on the development of phonics and word knowledge. In this activity, students use letters to create new words and to identify word patterns. The ability to identify letter–sound correspondence is critical to success in beginning reading. Children who are given multiple opportunities to practice letter–sound correspondence and to use this knowledge to decode unknown words are acquiring the foundation for literacy (Snow, Burns, & Griffin, 1998).

The National Reading Panel (2000) reported that there was substantial research on the importance of systematic phonics instruction in learning to read. The report also indicated that explicit phonics instruction led to improved reading comprehension as well. Reading comprehension improved due to the students' automatic word recognition skills, or *automaticity for word recognition*. Children who find it difficult to read often lack the required word knowledge to decode unknown words.

The Making Words strategy allows children to practice letter–sound correspondence and to transfer knowledge to unknown words. This activity is an example of direct instruction that leads to success in beginning reading success (Adams, 1990).

Learner Outcomes

- The students will identify letter–sound correspondence.
- The students will generate new words based on their knowledge of word patterns.
- The students will sort words into categories.

Instructional Procedure

The Making Words strategy helps students to develop decoding skills and to generate vocabulary. This activity can be done with the whole class, with small groups, and even individually. Intermediate grade students that are struggling with decoding may also benefit from this activity.

1. The teacher selects a key word to focus on during the activity. The teacher may want to select words that are based on a thematic unit or a certain word pattern.

2. Each student or pair of students is given a set of letter cards to complete the activity, such as this one:

3. The teacher uses a pocket chart with large-print letter cards to model the Making Words activity. English language learners and struggling readers might need color-coded cards to help identify letters and sounds.

4. The teacher directs the activity by asking the students to make two-, three-, four-, and five-letter words. This chart illustrates some of those words:

5. As the students make words, the teacher or students write the words on chart paper to record new vocabulary. Students can use this chart as a reference tool during independent writing.

6. The teacher then asks, "Who can use all the letters to make the secret word?" If the students cannot make the word, the teacher can guide them through the process by giving them clues.

rains

7. The conclusion of the activity is to sort the new words into categories. Teachers may include this as a center activity for students with attention-deficit problems.

8. When the students have finished the word sort activity, they glue the words to the worksheet in Figure 2.4 and present their rationales for the word categories. Students should compare their rationales and develop rules about word patterns as a summation of the activity.

Category	Category
Rationale for Categories:	

FIGURE 2.4: Word Categories

An Application of Making Words Strategy for Grade 2

Ms. Garcia has analyzed her students' assessment data and determined that they need additional help with decoding and blending sounds. In order to help facilitate her students' decoding skills, Ms. Garcia has decided to do the Making Words activity with them. The students have been reading *Charlotte's Web*, by E. B. White (1952) and enjoyed the many animal characters. Ms. Garcia has handed out letter cards to a small group of struggling readers.

1. The students name the letters on the magnetic board and line up the letter cards in front of them.

2. José takes his letter cards and is able to make these words:

3. All of the students in José's group excitedly call out their words, and Ms. Garcia writes their responses on chart paper. The chart will be placed on the board for the students to use as a reference. When the students return to their seats, they will write the words in their personal dictionaries.

4. At the end of the session, Ms. Garcia asks the students, "Can anyone guess the secret word?" Mark excitedly raises his hand and says, "I know what it is! The word is *animal*." The students return to their seats and write the words in their dictionaries. Victor has decided to illustrate his entry of *lima* and draws a lima bean.

Assessment Procedure

The Annotated Checklist for Vocabulary Acquisition (Figure 2.5) should be used to assess the readers' vocabulary development and identification of word patterns. The checklist can be used in its totality, or the teacher may want to use it developmentally over a period of time.

Step by Step

1. The teacher observes students during the Making Words activity. The teacher may want to particularly note if students struggle with certain patterns of words on a continuous basis.

2. Based on each student's performance, the teacher rates him or her as *beginning, developed, competent, proficient,* or *advanced*. The teacher enters the date the student has reached a particular level on the checklist.

   • Students are rated as *advanced* if they consistently perform above the benchmark behavior. The teacher should also note if the words need to be more challenging or if the students have achieved automaticity for word recognition.

   • A rating of *proficient* is given to students who perform the benchmark consistently in a variety of contexts. Students rated as *proficient* perform without support and do not make any errors.

	Date	Date	Date	Date	Date
Generation of Words Student can create a word and discuss its definition.					
Word Usage Student can use a word in the proper context.					
Rationale Student can describe reasoning for categorization of words.					

Annotated Checklist for Vocabulary Acquisition

Name _____   Date _____

OBSERVATION NOTES AND COMMENTS

SUMMARY OF STUDENT PERFORMANCE

FIGURE 2.5: Annotated Checklist for Vocabulary Acquisition

- Students are rated as *competent* if they demonstrate the benchmark skill the majority of the time. Students rated as *competent* may make a few errors.
- Students are rated as *developed* when they have partially mastered the behavior. Students who are rated as *developed* are still struggling with their decoding skills and need repeated practice in making words.
- Students are rated as *beginning* when they can only generate a few words on their own. Students who are rated as *beginning* require a great deal of scaffolding to perform the task.

Professional Resources to Explore

Center for the Improvement of Early Reading Achievement
www.ciera.org
This site provides teachers with research regarding emergent literacy and the development of decoding skills.

United States Department of Education
www.ed.gov
This federal government website offers links to research on decoding skills and evidence-based reading instruction.

Cunningham, P. M. (2000). *Phonics they use: Words for reading and writing* (3rd ed.). New York: Longman.

Cunningham, P. M., & Cunningham, J. W. (1992). Making words: Enhancing the invented spelling-decoding connection. *Reading Teacher, 46,* 106–107.

Lane, H. B., & Pullen, P. C. (2004). *Phonological awareness: Assessment and instruction.* Boston: Pearson.

References

Adams, M. J. (1990). *Beginning to read: Thinking and learning about print.* Cambridge, MA: MIT Press.

Cunningham, P. M., & Cunningham, J. W. (1992). Making words: Enhancing the invented spelling decoding connection. *Reading Teacher, 46,* 106–115.

National Reading Panel. (2000). *Teaching children to read: An evidence-based assessment of the scientific research literature on reading and its implications for reading instruction.* Washington, DC: U.S. Department of Health and Human Services.

Snow, K., Burns, M. S., & Griffin, P. (Eds.). (1998). *Preventing reading difficulties in young children.* Washington, DC: National Academy Press.

Children's Literature References

White, E. B. (1952). *Charlotte's web.* New York: Harper & Row.

A Strategy for Developing Reading Fluency

INSTRUCTIONAL CONTEXT				
Grade Level	*Literacy Level*	*Group Size*	*Literature Genre*	*Literacy Skills*
● K–1	● Emergent	● Whole class	● Fiction	● Comprehension
● 2–4	● Early	● 8–10 students	● Nonfiction	❖ Vocabulary
● 5–6	● Transitional	● 4–6 students		● Discussion
● 7–8	● Fluent	● Individual		● Writing
				● Critical thinking

● *Applicable*	○ *Not applicable*	❖ *Target skill*

A Framework for Instruction

The Repeated Readings strategy provides students with the opportunity to read a text aloud until they can read it fluently. Teachers who use this strategy provide direct instruction in reading fluency: accurate word recognition and pronunciation, suitable phrasing, using punctuation as guideposts, reading with expression, and an adequate reading rate. The books selected for the Repeated Readings strategy are those that students can read with meaning, have a high-interest level, and contain decodable words (when they are unfamiliar to the students). After students have had repeated readings of a text, they should experience success in reading that leads to higher levels of engagement with other books.

Researchers agree on the components of reading fluency: (1) word accuracy; (2) accurate phrasing of text; (3) reading with expression that includes appropriate use of pitch, juncture, and stress in the reader's voice (*reading prosody*); and (4) suitable rate of reading (Allington, 2001; National Reading Panel, 2000; Rasinski & Padak, 2001; Richards, 2001). All students need to be monitored and provided assistance in becoming fluent readers.

Although reading fluency is a major goal of early childhood teachers, beyond the primary grades, direct instruction in reading fluency and assessment is rarely considered part of the literacy program (Worthy & Broaddus, 2001/2002). It may be that teachers believe that when students become proficient in word recognition strategies, their rate of reading will be at the appropriate levels and their reading expression will improve, as will the prosodic features of pitch, juncture, and stress. However, this is not always the case. Many students in the middle grades can benefit from direct instruction in reading fluency (Rasinski & Padak, 2001). Allington's (2001) suggestion of the six ways that students may develop reading fluency may be found in Figure 2.6.

Learner Outcomes

- The students will demonstrate improved word recognition and pronunciation over repeated readings.
- The students will demonstrate improved oral reading rates over repeated readings.

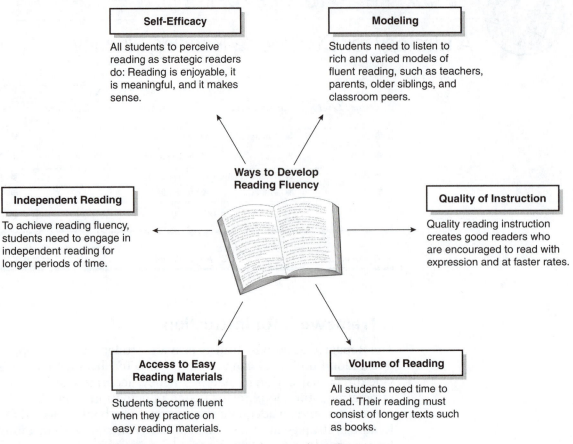

FIGURE 2.6: Ways to Develop Reading Fluency
Source: Based on Allington, 2001.

- The students will demonstrate improved phrasing oral reading over repeated readings.
- The students will demonstrate improved expression in oral reading over repeated readings.

Instructional Procedure

The use of the Repeated Reading strategy to offer students instruction in and assessment of oral reading fluency can be implemented in a variety of instructional contexts. For example, emergent readers in a primary classroom may be asked to reread a "big book" during shared reading several times, while older students engaged in literature circles may be asked to select a favorite passage or chapter from the book, reread it several times for fluency, and share it with their group through a read-aloud. The purpose of the Repeated Reading strategy remains the same for any instructional context: to assist and to monitor students in their development of oral reading fluency. In each case, students reread the passage several times to gain oral reading fluency.

Step by Step

1. The teacher selects a book that is at an appropriate reading level for the students. When beginning the Repeated Reading strategy, the teacher starts with shorter books or poems.

2. The teacher engages the students in reading the book and conducts a discussion of the story, ensuring students' comprehension of the text.

3. The teacher models reading aloud, showing expressive reading and how it is related to the meaning of the story. The teacher emphasizes the importance of stopping at punctuation marks and using sentence structure as a guide for slowing down, reading faster, and raising and lowering one's voice for expressive reading.

4. The students engage in repeated readings by reading the text several times. They may work with a partner or by themselves. The teacher monitors students for their reading fluency and may ask them to read the selection to their parents or siblings for additional practice.

5. The students read their selected passages to the group while the teacher assesses their oral reading fluency.

An Application of Repeated Readings for Grade 6

In Amanda Woodrow's sixth grade, the students are engaged in reading different poetry selections during literature circles. During the ninety-minute block of time, groups of children read, discuss, and write about poetry. Amanda is working with one small group of children who are struggling with oral reading fluency, especially lacking proficiency in word recognition skills. They are reading Shel Silverstein's (1974) *Where the Sidewalk Ends* and have decided that they will select their favorite poems and present them to the whole class through a poetry "read-in." They begin by discussing each of the poems that they select for the event, asking questions about words and meanings, responding to them in their journals, and reading their responses to each other in their literature circle.

To practice for their presentations, the students engage in repeated readings of their poems. They work in pairs, reading their poems to each other until they can read them smoothly, fast enough to hold their audience's attention, with expression, and with no errors in word recognition. They take their poems home and practice by reading to their families. When they are ready to present to the class, the group sits in the front of the classroom, facing their audience. Terry, the group leader, introduces the book, briefly describing some of the poems to the class. One by one, the group leader introduces each member, who reads his or her favorite poem to the class.

As the children perform for their friends, Amanda assesses their oral reading fluency. Figure 2.7 shows Jake's performance on the poem "Sick" (Silverstein, 1974, pp. 58–59). Amanda assessed his reading prior to the repeated readings as well as when he finished practicing.

Assessment Procedure

To profile students' oral reading, the teacher needs to listen to their oral reading on a regular basis to assess their word recognition and pronunciation skills, rate of reading, phrasing, reading expression, and tonal qualities.

Step by Step

1. *Assessing reading rate:* The teacher will assess the *rate of reading*, or the number of words the student reads in one minute (WPM).
   a. Using a stopwatch to monitor the time, the teacher sits close to the student and listens to him or her read. The teacher marks the text where the student reads and listens for one minute.

Assessment of Performance on Repeated Oral Readings

Name Jake   Grade 6[1]

WPM															
210															
200															
190															
180															
170															
160															
150															
140															
130															
120															
110															
100															
90															
80															
70															
60															
50															
40															
30															
20															
10															
DATE →	10/2	10/3	10/4												

WORD ACCURACY RATE

Date	# of Words	# of Errors	Word Accuracy Rate
10/2	100	13	87%
10/3	100	7	93%
10/4	100	1	99%

QUALITY OF ORAL READING
Interpretive Expression, Reading in Meaningful Phrases

Date	Level	Emergent Level of Oral Reading	Early Level of Oral Reading	Fluent Level of Oral Reading
10/2	Early	• Reads word-by-word	• Reads with three- or four-word groups	• Reads with some expressive interpretation
10/3	Early	• Advances to reading two- to three-word phrases	• Reads with small word groups but preserves the author's meaning and syntax	• Demonstrates reading for understanding through the use of larger and meaningful phrase groups
10/4	Fluent	• Lacks expression		• Reads with some repetitions or deviations from text but preserves the author's meaning and sentence structure

FIGURE 2.7: Jake's Oral Reading Performance

    b. When one minute is up, the teacher marks the text where the student finished and counts the number of words the student read.

    c. The teacher records the date and the number of words that the student read in one minute.

2. *Assessing other aspects of oral reading:* The teacher also listens to the *expression* in the student's reading as well as the *phrasing.* The teacher uses the rubric to determine the oral reading level for expressive reading and phrasing that the student demonstrates. After listening to the student read orally, the teacher decides whether the student demonstrates literacy behaviors at the emergent, early, or fluent level.

3. *Assessing word accuracy rate:* While the student is reading, the teacher listens to determine the number of words he or she reads correctly.

    a. Mark each word the student reads incorrectly.

    b. Mark the percentage of words that the student read correctly. For example, if the student read 97 words out of 100 words correctly, the word accuracy rate is 97 percent.

Professional Resources to Explore

Repeated Readings and Oral Reading Fluency Websites
www.readingcenter.buffalo.edu/center/research/tmgrr.html
This website provides a paper prepared by Michael W. Kibby on teacher modeling and guided repeated readings.

www.people.memphis.edu/~coe_rise/Debbs.html
This website presents a paper called "Video self-modeling as a tool for improving oral reading fluency and self-confidence."

Griffin, M. L. (2002). Why don't you use your finger? Paired reading in first grade. *Reading Teacher, 55*(8), 766–774.

Rathvon, N. (1999). *Effective school interventions.* New York: Guilford Press.

Samuels, J. (1997). The method of repeated readings. *Reading Teacher, 50*(5), 376–381.

References

Allington, R. L. (2001). *What really matters for struggling readers: Designing research-based programs.* New York: Addison-Wesley/Longman.

National Reading Panel. (2000). *Teaching children to read: An evidence-based assessment of the scientific research literature on reading and its implications for reading instruction.* Bethesda, MD: National Institutes of Health.

Rasinski, T., & Padak, N. (2001). *From phonics to fluency: Effective teaching of decoding and reading fluency in the elementary school.* New York: Longman.

Richards, M. (2001). Be a good detective: Solve the case of oral reading fluency. *Reading Teacher, 53*(7), 534–539.

Worthy, J., & Broaddus, K. (2001/2002). Fluency beyond the primary grades: From group performance to silent, independent read. *Reading Teacher, 55*(4), 334–342.

Children's Literature References

Silverstein, S. (1974). *Where the sidewalk ends.* New York: Harper & Row.

14 SEMANTIC MAPPING

A Strategy for Developing Word Meanings

INSTRUCTIONAL CONTEXT				
Grade Level	*Literacy Level*	*Group Size*	*Literature Genre*	*Literacy Skills*
● K–1	● Emergent	● Whole class	● Fiction	● Comprehension
● 2–4	● Early	● 8–10 students	● Nonfiction	❖ Vocabulary
● 5–6	● Transitional	● 4–6 students		● Discussion
● 7–8	● Fluent	● Individual		● Writing
				● Critical thinking

● *Applicable*	O *Not applicable*	❖ *Target skill*

A Framework for Instruction

The Semantic Mapping strategy is used for teaching students the relationship among words and their meanings. A *semantic map* is a graphic organizer that the teacher and students use to show the visual relationships among words. A *word map* is a diagram that organizes the related concepts under one or more categories and, through a series of lines, shows their relationships to other concepts. It is a "categorization procedure that organizes words related to a core concept into meaningful clusters" (Baumann & Kameenui, 1991, p. 615).

There are many ways of using a semantic map. A teacher may decide to ask students to provide the characteristics or describing features of a word concept, include examples and nonexamples, provide antonyms and synonyms, chart the causes and results, and so on. A critical aspect of the strategy is engaging students in discussion about the meanings of the words. During the teacher-led discussion of word meanings, the students are assisted in making connections to what they know about the words, as they record their understandings on semantic maps.

Teaching word meanings is one aspect of vocabulary development that goes beyond teaching students a set of dictionary definitions. A word may be thought of as a label for a concept, and for most concepts, there are multiple layers of meanings with varied dimensions of knowledge. Thus, learning word meanings is akin to knowledge acquisition. Further, McKeown and Beck (1988) argue that "word knowledge is not an all-or-nothing proposition. Words may be known at different levels" (p. 42). The Semantic Mapping strategy (Heimlich & Pittelman, 1986) facilitates students' deeper understanding of words, which goes beyond learning simple definitions. Using teacher-led discussions, students' conceptual knowledge of a word is increased by promoting activation of their prior knowledge related to the new word and helping to establish the semantic relatedness of words with similar meanings (Baumann & Kameenui, 1991).

The Semantic Mapping strategy is excellent for prediscussion and postdiscussion when reading literature and content-area textbooks. Students also may learn to use semantic mapping as a note-taking strategy for study or for research. Finally, it is an excellent approach for helping students organize their ideas prior to writing.

Learner Outcomes

- The students will participate in a prereading discussion on the target vocabulary words and use the semantic map for organizing their ideas.
- The students will add to their meanings of words using their semantic maps during reading.
- The students' final semantic maps will demonstrate an increased knowledge of words and their relationships, designed around meaningful clusters.

Instructional Procedure

There are many ways to use the Semantic Mapping strategy. One effective way is to create the pre- and postreading discussions around semantic maps. The prereading semantic map will encourage students to activate the prior knowledge that aids in comprehension and will help them realize that they need to learn more about the meanings of words for a deeper understanding of text. The postreading semantic map will serve as a visual representation of new word meanings and their relationships, which students have learned through reading and discussions. There are three phases to the instructional sequence: the prereading discussion phase, the reading phase, and the postreading discussion phase.

Step by Step

Prereading Discussion Phase

1. The teacher selects the word concepts from the books that the students will read. Teachers frequently select words that are related integrally to comprehending the readings and words that represent broad categories, where many conceptual relationships may be demonstrated.

2. Prior to reading, the teacher introduces the text to students by helping them make connections to their personal experiences. The prereading discussion will be based on the major concepts in the reading and include a discussion of the vocabulary of what students will be reading.

3. On a large sheet of chart paper, on the chalkboard, or on a transparency, the teacher draws a semantic map and writes a word in the center. Using the semantic map as a guide, the teacher begins a discussion of the major word concepts within the story.

4. The teacher poses questions to the students to guide the discussion. The guiding questions may be written on the semantic map. As students contribute to the discussion, they record the information under the appropriate question. The prereading map represents students' prior knowledge and should be used to set a purpose for reading and to acquire more knowledge of the word concepts found in the reading. The unanswered questions may help guide students as they read.

Reading Phase

1. The teacher directs students to read the selected text, reminding them of the questions that need answering. During this aspect of the strategy, the goal is to help students expand their knowledge of the vocabulary words from their reading.

2. The teacher may find it necessary to model how reading may answer some of the questions and build vocabulary knowledge. Show the students how to build their definitions around the words from their reading. Direct students to the words in the text that expand the meaning of a word, and demonstrate to students how these word explanations may be added to their semantic maps.

Postreading Discussion Phase

1. When students have completed their reading, the teacher guides the discussion, helping students to complete their semantic word maps, expanding word meanings, and showing relationships between words. An example of a postreading semantic word map may be found in Figure 2.8.

An Application of Semantic Maps for Grade 4

Students in Robert Wilson's fourth grade were engaged in a thematic unit entitled "The Unexplored." A portion of the unit included the study of inventions and inventors. Robert used the Semantic Mapping strategy to determine what the students knew prior to their unit and what they learned after their readings and activities on inventions. Figure 2.8 shows the Semantic Map on Inventions after the discussion.

Assessment Procedure

Assessment of students during the Semantic Mapping strategy may be conducted through the teacher's observation of students' participation during the discussion phases and their use of semantic maps. The teacher may analyze students' writing samples to determine their use of new vocabulary words.

Step by Step

To assess students' participation in discussion, the teacher observes them during the pre- and postdiscussions. The focus of the teacher's observation is each student's level of participation in the discussion. There are four levels of participation, from the lowest level, *Beginning (1)*, indicating no participation, to the highest level, *Advanced (4)*, denoting an active level of participation. Using the rubric as a guide in the description of each level, the teacher notes the student's level of participation in the discussion (see Figure 2.9):

1. The teacher observes the student writing on his or her semantic map. The teacher observes how the student uses the map and determines his or her level of competence. The focus of the teacher's observation is on understanding and the use of the semantic map during reading. The lowest level, *Beginning*, indicates that the student does not use the map during reading, and the highest level, *Advanced*, indicates that the student goes far beyond the recording of new meanings to developing new relationships and adding new words.

2. The teacher examines the student's semantic map and listens to how he or she uses the words in discussions to determine his or her level of word knowledge. The lowest level of word knowledge, *Beginning*, indicates that the student does not use the new words in speaking or writing, and the highest level of word knowledge, *Advanced*, shows that the student uses all of the new words with accuracy during reading and writing.

3. The teacher records the names of the students who are using semantic maps and participating in the discussion. Using the rubric to guide the assess-

FIGURE 2.8: Semantic Map on Inventions

ment, the teacher evaluates the following aspects of literacy skills for each student: (a) level of participation in the discussion, (b) understanding and use of the semantic map during reading, and (c) word knowledge.

Professional Resources to Explore

Semantic Mapping Website
www.allamericareads.org/lessonplan/strategies/vocab/mapping.html
This website will provide the reader with a sample lesson, a procedure for using semantic webs, and a sample graphic to help implement the lesson.

Allen, J. (1999). *Words, words, words: Teaching vocabulary in Grades 4–12*. Portland, ME: Stenhouse.

Assessment of Vocabulary Development Using Semantic Mapping

Students' Names	Discussion: Level of Participation				Use of Semantic Map				Word Knowledge			
1.	1	2	3	4	1	2	3	4	1	2	3	4
2.	1	2	3	4	1	2	3	4	1	2	3	4
3.	1	2	3	4	1	2	3	4	1	2	3	4
4.	1	2	3	4	1	2	3	4	1	2	3	4
5.	1	2	3	4	1	2	3	4	1	2	3	4
6.	1	2	3	4	1	2	3	4	1	2	3	4
7.	1	2	3	4	1	2	3	4	1	2	3	4
8.	1	2	3	4	1	2	3	4	1	2	3	4
9.	1	2	3	4	1	2	3	4	1	2	3	4
10.	1	2	3	4	1	2	3	4	1	2	3	4
11.	1	2	3	4	1	2	3	4	1	2	3	4
12.	1	2	3	4	1	2	3	4	1	2	3	4

A Rubric for Vocabulary Development through Semantic Mapping

	Beginning 1	Developing 2	Proficient 3	Advanced 4
Level of Participation	There is no participation during discussion. The student offers no contributions to the pre- or post-discussion.	The student participates on a minimal basis, making few contributions to the pre- and post-discussions.	The student participates on a regular basis, making good contributions to the pre- and post-discussions.	The student is an active participant in both discussions; he or she makes insightful contributions that stimulate the discussion as new information is offered.
Use of Semantic Map	The student does not understand how to use the semantic map.	The student uses the semantic word map with assistance.	The student uses the semantic word map with no assistance.	The student goes beyond the basic semantic map, adding new words and developing new relationships.
Word Knowledge	The student does not use new words in speaking or writing. The semantic map does not indicate that the student added new words or meanings after reading and from the discussion.	The student uses very few new words in speaking or writing. Some words are not used accurately. Some new words and meanings were added to the semantic map.	The student uses some new words accurately in speaking and writing. A moderate amount of new words and meanings were added to the semantic map after reading and discussing.	The student uses most of the new words during the discussions as well as in writing. Words are used accurately. Many new words with descriptive meanings are added to the semantic map after reading and participating in the discussion.

FIGURE 2.9: Assessment of Vocabulary Development Using Semantic Mapping

Brand, M., & Deford, D. (2004). *Word savvy: Integrating vocabulary, spelling, and word study, Grades 3–6.* Portland, ME: Stenhouse.

Duffelmeyer, F. A. (1985). Teaching word meaning from an experience base. *Reading Teacher, 38,* 6–11.

Schwartz, R. M. (1988). Learning to learn vocabulary in content area textbooks. *Journal of Reading, 32,* 108–118.

Schwartz, R. M., & Raphael, T. E. (1985). Concept definition: A key to improving students' vocabulary. *Reading Teacher, 39,* 198–205.

References

Baumann, J. F., & Kameenui, E. J. (1991). Research on vocabulary instruction: Ode to Voltaire. In J. Flood, J. M. Jensen, D. Lapp, & J. R. Squire (Eds.), *Handbook of research on teaching the English language arts* (pp. 604–632). New York: Macmillan.

Heimlich, J. E., & Pittelman, S. D. (1986). *Semantic mapping: Classroom applications.* Newark, DE: International Reading Association.

McKeown, M., & Beck, I. (1988). Learning vocabulary: Different ways for different goals. *Remedial and Special Education, 9*(1), 42–46.

A Strategy for Developing Word Knowledge

INSTRUCTIONAL CONTEXT				
Grade Level	**Literacy Level**	**Group Size**	**Literature Genre**	**Literacy Skills**
● K–2	● Emergent	● Whole class	● Fiction	● Comprehension
● 2–4	● Early	● 8–10 students	○ Nonfiction	❖ Vocabulary
○ 5–6	○ Transitional	● 4–6 students		● Discussion
○ 7–8	○ Fluent	○ Individual		● Writing
				● Critical thinking

● *Applicable*	○ *Not applicable*	❖ *Target skill*

A Framework for Instruction

The Word Book strategy provides a natural extension activity during literature study or a thematic unit. In this strategy, students create their own dictionaries based on books they are reading or on units of study. As students create their own dictionaries, they are actively engaged in word study and make connections between concepts that research has found to be critical for vocabulary development (Blachowicz & Fisher, 2000). Research on effective vocabulary instruction has found that when students choose their own words to study during literature units, they select difficult words and retain their definitions (Dole, Sloan, & Trathen, 1995; Fisher, Blachowicz, & Smith, 1991).

Word books also become reference tools for students to look up words as they write or read daily in the classroom. As students refer to words repeatedly and use them in their writing assignments, they are engaging in the three critical components of vocabulary instruction as, defined by Nagy (1988):

- *Integration*—New concepts or words are integrated into the existing knowledge base.
- *Repetition*—Students use words repeatedly through reading and writing activities and begin to recognize words automatically.
- *Meaningful use*—Words are not learned in isolation but in context.

Word books can be used across the curriculum as students create reference tools for books about sharks, the American Revolution, or numbers. The following procedure describes how to implement this effective instructional strategy.

Learner Outcomes

- The students will create word books by choosing words they want to study.
- The students will use their word books as a reference tool for writing and reading tasks.
- The students will define words and relate them to other concepts.

Instructional Procedure

Word books may be created as part of a literature study or a thematic unit. For example, if students are studying colonial America, they can create a word book of concepts related to the unit. This Procedure section will use the unit on colonial America to illustrate how to implement this strategy.

Step by Step

1. Before students begin the unit of study, they can create a concept map of words they already know related to colonial America. English language learners might need more preparation for the content of the lesson.

2. Before the students begin their word books, the teacher models the process by demonstrating how to read a selection and choose words for study. For example, the teacher might say, "I will write the word *fishmonger* in my book because I don't know what it means. I will reread the sentence to see if I can figure it out from the context clues. After reading it, I realize now it must mean someone who sold fish in shops in colonial America."

3. The teacher then demonstrates on chart paper how to create a word book page. A sample is shown in Figure 2.10.

4. The students then begin to create their own word books by choosing three words. As the children read and study concepts from the unit, they expand their word books to include new words.

5. As the students read and write daily, they are encouraged to use their word books as reference materials. As students use their word books, they should be encouraged to suggest words of their own to be studied.

6. The students may choose to finalize their word books by using the computer to print out pages and create images to accompany each word. Students

FIGURE 2.10: Sample Word Book Page

with dyslexia might find the typing of words very helpful in identifying words.

7. After the unit or literature study has been completed, the students can add new words to the original concept map that was started at the beginning of the unit (see Figure 2.11). The students may construct a summation chart of their new knowledge in regard to vocabulary.

An Application of Word Books for Grade 3

Ms. Sanabria's third-grade class began a literature study on fables. As an introduction to the topic, Ms. Sanabria asked the class what they already knew about fables. The students provided several characteristics of fables, and Ms. Sanabria recorded their responses on chart paper, as shown here:

> **CHARACTERISTICS OF FABLES**
>
> Fables cannot happen.
>
> There are lots of animals.
>
> Fables teach lessons.
>
> There might be some magic.

The students next created a concept map of words they associated with fables and discussed what they knew about each vocabulary term.

When the students finished discussing the concept map about fables, Ms. Sanabria asked them to select three new terms and to create entries in their word books. Paul was interested in animals, so he decided to focus on the terms *hare*, *troll*, and *beasts*. Paul's word book entry for *troll* is illustrated

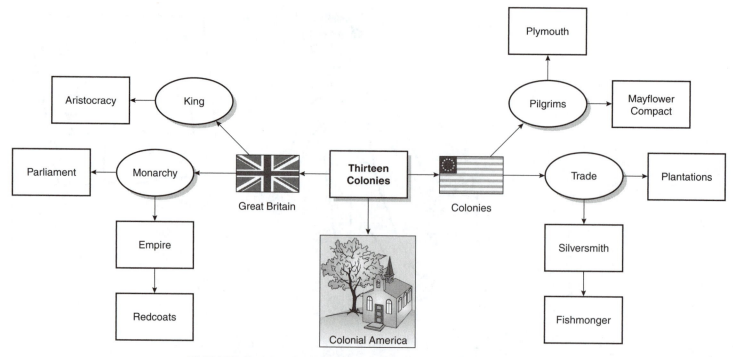

FIGURE 2.11: Concept Map after the Word Book

FIGURE 2.12: Sample Word Book Page

in Figure 2.12. Paul used his word book to write his own story, entitled "The Hare and the Troll."

Assessment Procedure

As the students create and use their word books, the teacher can use the checklist illustrated in Figure 2.13 to mark his or her observations. The form may be used developmentally to record students' progress with new vocabulary words over the semester.

Step by Step

1. As the students create their concept maps and word books, teachers observe their performance. Teachers may want to focus on how students use their prior knowledge or context clues to define new vocabulary words.

2. Teachers focus their observations by rating students on the benchmark behaviors. Teachers may choose to modify the form to add other skills or strategies that are pertinent to the literature study or thematic unit.

   • Students are rated as *Advanced* if they consistently perform above the benchmark behavior. Teachers should also note if the words need to be

Annotated Checklist of Word Knowledge

Name _____ Date _____

Literacy Behaviors	Beginning	Developed	Competent	Proficient	Advanced
Definitions of Words Student is able to define word and discuss concept.					
Word Usage Student uses word in proper context.					
Reference Student uses word book as reference tool for reading and writing.					

OBSERVATION NOTES AND COMMENTS

SUMMARY OF PERFORMANCE

FIGURE 2.13: Assessment of Word Knowledge

more challenging or if the students have achieved automaticity for word recognition.

- A rating of *Proficient* is given to students who perform the benchmark consistently in a variety of contexts. Students rated as *Proficient* easily complete their word books without any support.
- Students are rated as *Competent* if they demonstrate the benchmark skill the majority of the time. Students rated as *Competent* may make a few errors in their word books.
- Students are rated as *Developed* when they have partially mastered the behavior. Students who are rated as *Developed* are still struggling with their decoding skills and need repeated practice in making words.
- Students are rated as *Beginning* when they can only generate a few words on their own. Students who are rated as *Beginning* require a great deal of scaffolding to perform the task.

Category	Category
short *a*	long *a*
ham	gave
pat	save
can	tame
Why did you group them that way?	
One group had short vowels, and the other had long vowels.	

FIGURE 2.16: Word Sort Worksheet

An Application of the Word Sort Strategy for Grade 1

It is Monday morning, and Ms. Vargas has prepared a Word Sort activity for her first-grade class to perform during their two-hour literacy block. The students are struggling to learn the differences between long and short vowels. Many of the first-graders are English language learners, for whom decoding long and short vowel sounds continues to be a problem. Ms. Vargas invites a small group to come to the meeting area for the word study lesson. She gives the children the following words on stick-on notes: *gave, ham, tame, save, pat.*

The students work in pairs to move their words around and decide on categories. When the students have completed their discussion, they complete the worksheet shown in Figure 2.16.

Assessment Procedure

The purpose of the Annotated Rating Scale for Vocabulary Acquisition (see Figure 2.17) is to assess the reader's vocabulary development and identification of word patterns. The teacher may note the student's performance in this activity as compared to other strategies to discern the best mode of learning for further instruction.

p by Step

1. The teacher observes the students' behavior in the word sort activity. The teacher should note the students' rationales for sorting words.

2. As students perform the activity, use the rating scale to focus their observations. The rating scale can be modified for group observations, as well.

3. If students demonstrate beyond the benchmark behavior consistently, they are rated as *Advanced.* The student is rated as *Proficient* when he or she masters the task. When the behavior is primarily consistent, the teacher rates the performance as *Competent.* Students who partially perform the task or are inconsistent are rated as *Developing.* When students need assistance to perform the task, they are rated as *Beginning.*

4. The Annotated Rating Scale for Vocabulary Acquisition should be used developmentally over the academic year so that progress is noted. The teacher should especially note students' development of vocabulary knowledge as well as identification of word patterns.

Professional Resources to Explore

Four Blocks Literacy Model
www.wfu.edu/-cunningh/fourblocks
This site offers help in lesson planning and decoding skills activities.

The Teacher's Toolbox
www.trc.org/toolbox.html
This site provides multiple links to literacy websites as well as sites for generating rubrics.

Cunningham, P. (1990). The names test: A quick assessment of decoding ability. *Reading Teacher, 46,* 106–107.

Ehri, L. C., & McCormick, S. (1998). Phases of word learning implications for instruction with delayed and disabled readers. *Reading and Writing Quarterly: Overcoming Learning Disabilities, 14,* 135–163.

Phenix, J. (2004). *The spelling teacher's book of lists.* Portland, ME: Stenhouse.

References

Blachowicz, C. L., & Fisher, P. J. (2000). Vocabulary instruction. In M. Kamil, P. B. Mosenthal, P. D. Pearson, & R. Barr (Eds.), *Handbook of reading research* (Vol. 3, pp. 503–525). Mahwah, NJ: Erlbaum.

Dole, J. A., Sloan, C., & Trathen, W. (1995). Teaching vocabulary within the context of literature. *Journal of Reading, 38,* 452–460.

Fisher, P. J., Blachowicz, C. L., & Smith, J. C. (1991). Vocabulary learning in literature discussion groups. In J. Zutell & S. McCormick (Eds.), *Learner factors/teacher factors: Issues in literacy research and instruction. Fortieth yearbook of the National Reading Conference* (pp. 201–209). Chicago, IL: National Reading Conference.

Nagy, W. E. (1988). *Teaching vocabulary to improve reading comprehension.* Newark, DE: International Reading Association.

16 WORD SORTS

A Strategy for Developing Word-Solving Skills

	INSTRUCTIONAL CONTEXT			
Grade Level	*Literacy Level*	*Group Size*	*Literature Genre*	*Literacy Skills*
● K–2	● Emergent	● Whole class	● Fiction	● Comprehension
● 2–4	● Early	● 8–10 students	○ Nonfiction	❖ Vocabulary
○ 5–6	○ Transitional	● 4–6 students		● Discussion
○ 7–8	○ Fluent	○ Individual		● Writing
				● Critical thinking

● *Applicable*	○ *Not applicable*	❖ *Target skill*

A Framework for Instruction

The Word Sort strategy allows children to expand their vocabulary knowledge by grouping words according to specific categories (Bear, Invernizzi, Templeton, & Johnston, 2000). When students group words according to themes, they are identifying common patterns. As students actively engage with words, they increase their lexicon, which leads to improved reading comprehension (Blachowicz & Fisher, 2000).

Effective vocabulary instruction uses active engagement to develop students' motivation to learn new words. In 2000, the National Reading Panel called for a variety of vocabulary strategies that incorporated personal engagement with words. Research has also indicated that repeated exposure to words in a variety of contexts is critical to increased vocabulary usage (Blachowicz & Fisher, 2000).

The Word Sort strategy can also be used to develop word study skills when children are asked to categorize words according to word patterns rather than meaning (Fountas & Pinnell, 1996). Similar to word sorts based on definitions, teachers can give children the word pattern or ask them to discern the category. Identifying word patterns is especially important for emergent and early readers to gain fluency. The following section will describe how to implement this versatile strategy.

Learner Outcomes

- The students will group words according to a theme or word pattern.
- The students will defend their choices of categories to their peers.

Instructional Procedure

The Word Sort strategy facilitates development of word recognition skills and helps students to develop fluency. This activity is especially useful for struggling readers that need to develop a greater awareness of word patterns. The Word Sorts activity can be implemented across grade or ability levels.

Step by Step

1. After the students have finished reading a chapter in their textbook or another book, the teacher models the Word Sort activity for the class. The teacher selects words for the activity based on the needs of the students.

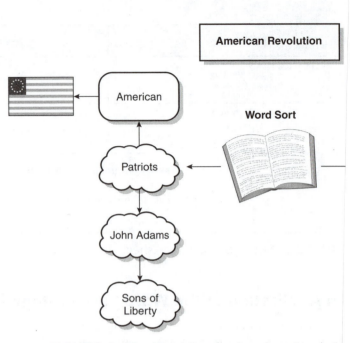

FIGURE 2.14: Word Sort for American Revolutio...

2. To model the activity, the teacher can write ... stick-on notes so the students can move the... teacher asks the students to identify why w... cific categories.

3. For example, after the students have read the... Revolution, they can begin a word sort (see...

4. After the teacher has modeled the activity, ... in groups to sort their own categories of wor... dents heterogeneously if there are strugglin...

5. When the students have finished the Word S... to the worksheet provided in Figure 2.15 a... their word categories.

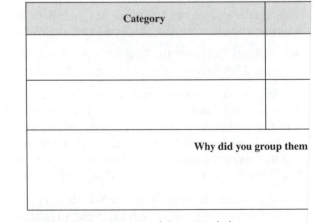

Category	
Why did you group them	

FIGURE 2.15: Word Sort Worksheet

Annotated Rating Scale for Vocabulary Acquisition Using Word Sorts

Name _____   Date _____

Word Sort Category _____

Benchmark Behaviors	1 ————— 5 Beginning Proficient	Comments
Identification of Words Student defines word, gives examples, and discusses concept.		
Word Usage Student uses word in proper context.		
Lexicon Student relates new word or concept to prior knowledge.		
Rationale Student is able to describe reasoning for categorization of words.		

SUMMARY OF PERFORMANCE

FIGURE 2.17: Annotated Rating Scale for Vocabulary Acquisition Using Word Sorts

Professional Resources to Explore

Literacy.org
www.literacy.org
This site provides teachers with activities to develop word knowledge.

Kathy Schrock's Guide for Educators
www.kathyschrock.net
Links are provided to lesson plans and decoding skill activities.

Brand, M., & Deford, D. (2004). *Word savvy: Integrating vocabulary, spelling, and word study, grades 3–6.* Portland, ME: Stenhouse.

Cunningham, P. M. (2000). *Phonics they use: Words for reading and writing* (3rd ed.). New York: Longman.

Heilman, A. W. (1998). *Phonics in proper perspective* (8th ed.). Upper Saddle River, NJ: Merrill.

References

Bear, D. R., Invernizzi, M., Templeton, S., & Johnston, F. (2000). *Words their way: Word study for phonics, vocabulary, and spelling instruction* (2nd ed.). Upper Saddle River, NJ: Prentice Hall/Merrill.

Blachowicz, C. L., & Fisher, P. (2000). Vocabulary instruction. In M. L. Kamil, P. B. Mosenthal, P. D. Pearson, & R. Barr (Eds.), *Handbook of Reading Research* (Vol. 3, pp. 503–525). Mahwah, NJ: Erlbaum.

Fountas, I. C., & Pinnell, G. S. (1996). *Guided reading: Good first teaching for all children.* Portsmouth, NH: Heinemann.

National Reading Panel. (2000). *Teaching children to read: An evidence-based assessment of the scientific research literature on reading and its implications for reading instruction.* Washington, DC: U.S. Department of Health and Human Services.

Professional Resources to Explore

Four Blocks Literacy Model
www.wfu.edu/-cunningh/fourblocks
This site offers help in lesson planning and decoding skills activities.

The Teacher's Toolbox
www.trc.org/toolbox.html
This site provides multiple links to literacy websites as well as sites for generating rubrics.

Cunningham, P. (1990). The names test: A quick assessment of decoding ability. *Reading Teacher, 46,* 106–107.

Ehri, L. C., & McCormick, S. (1998). Phases of word learning implications for instruction with delayed and disabled readers. *Reading and Writing Quarterly: Overcoming Learning Disabilities, 14,* 135–163.

Phenix, J. (2004). *The spelling teacher's book of lists.* Portland, ME: Stenhouse.

References

Blachowicz, C. L., & Fisher, P. J. (2000). Vocabulary instruction. In M. Kamil, P. B. Mosenthal, P. D. Pearson, & R. Barr (Eds.), *Handbook of reading research* (Vol. 3, pp. 503–525). Mahwah, NJ: Erlbaum.

Dole, J. A., Sloan, C., & Trathen, W. (1995). Teaching vocabulary within the context of literature. *Journal of Reading, 38,* 452–460.

Fisher, P. J., Blachowicz, C. L., & Smith, J. C. (1991). Vocabulary learning in literature discussion groups. In J. Zutell & S. McCormick (Eds.), *Learner factors/teacher factors: Issues in literacy research and instruction. Fortieth yearbook of the National Reading Conference* (pp. 201–209). Chicago, IL: National Reading Conference.

Nagy, W. E. (1988). *Teaching vocabulary to improve reading comprehension.* Newark, DE: International Reading Association.

A Strategy for Developing Word-Solving Skills

INSTRUCTIONAL CONTEXT				
Grade Level	*Literacy Level*	*Group Size*	*Literature Genre*	*Literacy Skills*
● K–2	● Emergent	● Whole class	● Fiction	● Comprehension
● 2–4	● Early	● 8–10 students	○ Nonfiction	❖ Vocabulary
○ 5–6	○ Transitional	● 4–6 students		● Discussion
○ 7–8	○ Fluent	○ Individual		● Writing
				● Critical thinking

● *Applicable*	○ *Not applicable*	❖ *Target skill*

A Framework for Instruction

The Word Sort strategy allows children to expand their vocabulary knowledge by grouping words according to specific categories (Bear, Invernizzi, Templeton, & Johnston, 2000). When students group words according to themes, they are identifying common patterns. As students actively engage with words, they increase their lexicon, which leads to improved reading comprehension (Blachowicz & Fisher, 2000).

Effective vocabulary instruction uses active engagement to develop students' motivation to learn new words. In 2000, the National Reading Panel called for a variety of vocabulary strategies that incorporated personal engagement with words. Research has also indicated that repeated exposure to words in a variety of contexts is critical to increased vocabulary usage (Blachowicz & Fisher, 2000).

The Word Sort strategy can also be used to develop word study skills when children are asked to categorize words according to word patterns rather than meaning (Fountas & Pinnell, 1996). Similar to word sorts based on definitions, teachers can give children the word pattern or ask them to discern the category. Identifying word patterns is especially important for emergent and early readers to gain fluency. The following section will describe how to implement this versatile strategy.

Learner Outcomes

- The students will group words according to a theme or word pattern.
- The students will defend their choices of categories to their peers.

Instructional Procedure

The Word Sort strategy facilitates development of word recognition skills and helps students to develop fluency. This activity is especially useful for struggling readers that need to develop a greater awareness of word patterns. The Word Sorts activity can be implemented across grade or ability levels.

Step by Step

1. After the students have finished reading a chapter in their textbook or another book, the teacher models the Word Sort activity for the class. The teacher selects words for the activity based on the needs of the students.

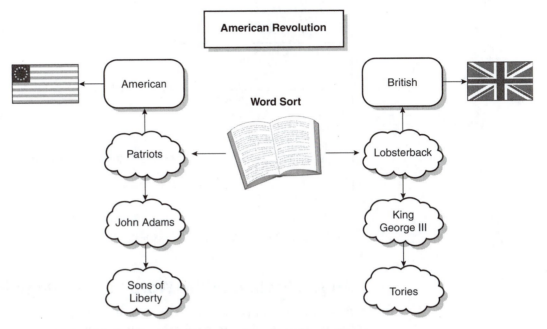

FIGURE 2.14: Word Sort for American Revolution

2. To model the activity, the teacher can write the words on transparencies or stick-on notes so the students can move them around into categories. The teacher asks the students to identify why words are being sorted into specific categories.

3. For example, after the students have read their first chapter on the American Revolution, they can begin a word sort (see Figure 2.14).

4. After the teacher has modeled the activity, the students can begin to work in groups to sort their own categories of words. The teacher should pair students heterogeneously if there are struggling readers in the class.

5. When the students have finished the Word Sort activity, they glue the words to the worksheet provided in Figure 2.15 and present their rationales for their word categories.

Category	Category
Why did you group them that way?	

FIGURE 2.15: Word Sort Worksheet

Category	Category
short *a*	long *a*
ham pat can	gave save tame

Why did you group them that way?

One group had short vowels, and the other had long vowels.

FIGURE 2.16: Word Sort Worksheet

An Application of the Word Sort Strategy for Grade 1

It is Monday morning, and Ms. Vargas has prepared a Word Sort activity for her first-grade class to perform during their two-hour literacy block. The students are struggling to learn the differences between long and short vowels. Many of the first-graders are English language learners, for whom decoding long and short vowel sounds continues to be a problem. Ms. Vargas invites a small group to come to the meeting area for the word study lesson. She gives the children the following words on stick-on notes: *gave, ham, tame, save, pat.*

The students work in pairs to move their words around and decide on categories. When the students have completed their discussion, they complete the worksheet shown in Figure 2.16.

Assessment Procedure

The purpose of the Annotated Rating Scale for Vocabulary Acquisition (see Figure 2.17) is to assess the reader's vocabulary development and identification of word patterns. The teacher may note the student's performance in this activity as compared to other strategies to discern the best mode of learning for further instruction.

Step by Step

1. The teacher observes the students' behavior in the word sort activity. The teacher should note the students' rationales for sorting words.

2. As students perform the activity, use the rating scale to focus their observations. The rating scale can be modified for group observations, as well.

3. If students demonstrate beyond the benchmark behavior consistently, they are rated as *Advanced.* The student is rated as *Proficient* when he or she masters the task. When the behavior is primarily consistent, the teacher rates the performance as *Competent.* Students who partially perform the task or are inconsistent are rated as *Developing.* When students need assistance to perform the task, they are rated as *Beginning.*

4. The Annotated Rating Scale for Vocabulary Acquisition should be used developmentally over the academic year so that progress is noted. The teacher should especially note students' development of vocabulary knowledge as well as identification of word patterns.

Annotated Rating Scale for Vocabulary Acquisition Using Word Sorts

Name _____   Date _____

Word Sort Category _____

Benchmark Behaviors	1 ———— 5 Beginning Proficient	Comments
Identification of Words Student defines word, gives examples, and discusses concept.		
Word Usage Student uses word in proper context.		
Lexicon Student relates new word or concept to prior knowledge.		
Rationale Student is able to describe reasoning for categorization of words.		

SUMMARY OF PERFORMANCE

FIGURE 2.17: Annotated Rating Scale for Vocabulary Acquisition Using Word Sorts

Professional Resources to Explore

Literacy.org
www.literacy.org
This site provides teachers with activities to develop word knowledge.

Kathy Schrock's Guide for Educators
www.kathyschrock.net
Links are provided to lesson plans and decoding skill activities.

Brand, M., & Deford, D. (2004). *Word savvy: Integrating vocabulary, spelling, and word study, grades 3–6.* Portland, ME: Stenhouse.

Cunningham, P. M. (2000). *Phonics they use: Words for reading and writing* (3rd ed.). New York: Longman.

Heilman, A. W. (1998). *Phonics in proper perspective* (8th ed.). Upper Saddle River, NJ: Merrill.

References

Bear, D. R., Invernizzi, M., Templeton, S., & Johnston, F. (2000). *Words their way: Word study for phonics, vocabulary, and spelling instruction* (2nd ed.). Upper Saddle River, NJ: Prentice Hall/Merrill.

Blachowicz, C. L., & Fisher, P. (2000). Vocabulary instruction. In M. L. Kamil, P. B. Mosenthal, P. D. Pearson, & R. Barr (Eds.), *Handbook of Reading Research* (Vol. 3, pp. 503–525). Mahwah, NJ: Erlbaum.

Fountas, I. C., & Pinnell, G. S. (1996). *Guided reading: Good first teaching for all children.* Portsmouth, NH: Heinemann.

National Reading Panel. (2000). *Teaching children to read: An evidence-based assessment of the scientific research literature on reading and its implications for reading instruction.* Washington, DC: U.S. Department of Health and Human Services.

Instructional and Assessment Strategies for Developing WRITING

Within this section are strategies to help students develop their writing. Although the emphasis is on writing instruction and assessment, the students will be involved in using other forms of language to complete each activity.

A Strategy for Developing Critical Thinking and Writing

INSTRUCTIONAL CONTEXT				
Grade Level	*Literacy Level*	*Group Size*	*Literature Genre*	*Literacy Skills*
○ K–2	○ Emergent	● Whole class	○ Fiction	● Comprehension
● 2–4	● Early	● 8–10 students	● Nonfiction	● Vocabulary
● 5–6	● Transitional	● 4–6 students		● Discussion
● 7–8	● Fluent	○ Individual		❖ Writing
				● Critical thinking

● *Applicable*	○ *Not applicable*	❖ *Target skill*

A Framework for Instruction

The Biography Writing strategy is an excellent instructional activity to help students interpret expository text and to make personal connections. Students select a famous person or hero about whom to write a biography for class presentation. When students research their persons' histories, they are speaking, reading, writing, and listening to expand their knowledge base. When students use language to write about historical personalities, the knowledge learned through one domain is transferred to another (Morrow, Pressley, Smith, & Smith, 1997). Biographical studies are also powerful tools for students to learn about different cultures and ideas while improving their language skills (Taylor, 2002).

Students that use the integrated language arts to write their biographies will expand and elaborate their knowledge base and their awareness of expository text formats (Antonacci & O'Callaghan, 2004). Additionally, as students develop the ability to write expository texts, their reading comprehension of these text formats will also improve (Tierney & Shanahan, 1991). When reading and writing instruction are integrated, both areas improve more than when either domain is presented alone (Armbruster & Osborn, 2002; Braunger & Lewis, 1997).

This section will illustrate how to implement this strategy across the curriculum as well as throughout the grades.

Learner Outcomes

- The students will write about a historical figure.
- The students will analyze a biographical figure and define his or her traits.
- The students will compare/contrast biographical figures.

Instructional Procedure

The Biography Writing strategy is designed to help children investigate famous figures and to discuss cultural differences. This strategy should be modeled by the teacher before students work on it independently.

Step by Step

1. The teacher begins by showing the class pictures of famous historical figures and explains why they are famous. The teacher may limit historical figures to those from units the students are currently studying, such as colonial America.

2. The students may research historical figures within the selected time period. Some students may need support in selecting a famous person to write about.

3. After they have selected historical figures, students use the following focus questions to conduct their research:

FOCUS QUESTIONS

1. When did your person live and where?
2. Why is he or she famous?
3. What did he or she do that you admire?
4. What traits did the person have that helped or hindered him or her?

---

4. After the students have researched their historical figures, they can analyze these individuals' traits with a graphic organizer.

5. After the students have defined the character traits for their famous figures, they write their biographies. The students may need a model or outline in order to begin their biographies.

6. After the students have shared their biographies, they meet in small groups to share what traits their historical figures had in common. Another graphic, called a *Venn diagram*, can be used to show the figures' common traits.

An Application of the Biography Writing Strategy for Grade 5

A fifth-grade class in Arlington, Massachusetts, had been studying the American Revolution. Ms. Cummins, the teacher, took the class on a field trip to John Adams's house in Quincy, and the students enjoyed looking at his humble home. Juan was especially interested in the farmhouse, since his family had a farm in the Dominican Republic. When Ms. Cummins announced that they could select their own famous person for biography writing, Juan selected John Adams.

Juan researched his historical figure on the Internet and in the school library. He used the focus questions Ms. Cummins gave the class to look for information about John Adams:

FOCUS QUESTIONS

1. When did your person live and where?
   John Adams lived in Quincy, Massachusetts, during the American Revolution.
2. Why is he or she famous?
   John Adams was one of the Founding Fathers and helped to win our independence.
3. What did he or she do that you admire?
   John Adams was a lawyer and he helped to write the Declaration of Independence.
4. What traits did the person have that helped or hindered him or her?
   John Adams was very brave. He also had a bad temper, just like me.

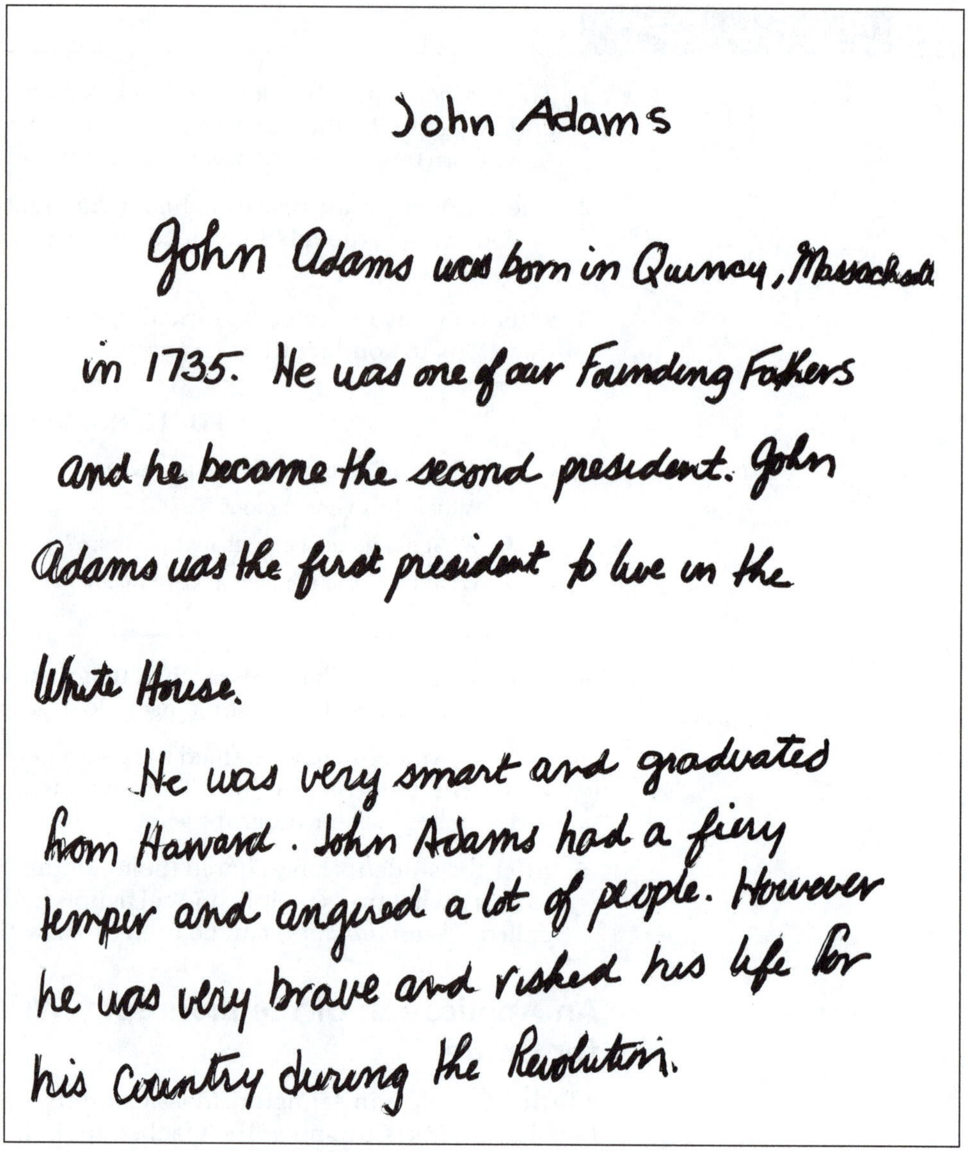

> ## John Adams
>
> John Adams was born in Quincy, Massachusetts in 1735. He was one of our Founding Fathers and he became the second president. John Adams was the first president to live in the White House.
>
> He was very smart and graduated from Haward. John Adams had a fiery temper and angered a lot of people. However he was very brave and risked his life for his Country during the Revolution.

FIGURE 3.1: Juan's Biography

After Juan finished the focus questions, he completed his graphic organizer on John Adams. Doing so helped Juan to select his thoughts for his biography, which is illustrated in Figure 3.1.

Assessment Procedure

The teacher should use the Rubric for Assessing Written Biographies (Figure 3.2) to guide him or her in analyzing students' written biographies. The form may be used developmentally to see how students progress over the academic year or in certain units.

Step by Step

1. The teacher observes students' literacy behaviors throughout the activity. English language learners may need more support during the initial components of the strategy, if they are recent immigrants to the United States.

Rubric for Assessing Written Biographies

Name _____   Date _____

Biography Elements	Beginning	Developing	Proficient
Famous Figure	Reference is made to famous person with little or no description.	Famous person is briefly described, with traits mentioned.	Famous person is thoroughly described, clearly relating character traits to life events.
Life Events	One or two life events are mentioned with no relation to whole life story.	Some life story events are mentioned. May be out of sequence.	Life story events are clearly described with a logical sequence.
Analysis of Famous Figure	No analysis of person is included.	Analysis is partial with some support for argument.	Famous person's life is fully analyzed with supporting argument.
Writing	**Beginning**	**Developing**	**Proficient**
Vocabulary	Vocabulary is simple with some inaccuracies. No new words are introduced.	Some descriptive words are used. One or two words from book are used.	Vocabulary is rich and elaborate.
Sentence Structure	Sentence structure is simplistic with many errors.	Sentences may contain some grammatical errors.	Sentence structure is correct and elaborate.
Spelling	Many spelling errors appear; misspelled words are not aligned to standard spelling.	Some errors that are not close to standard spelling.	A few errors in spelling; misspelled words are closely aligned to standard spelling.
Punctuation	Many errors in periods and question marks. No attempt is made at using commas.	A few errors in use of periods and question marks. Some attempt at using commas is made.	Rarely makes errors in punctuation.

FIGURE 3.2: Rubric for Assessing Written Biographies

The teacher may want to pair recent immigrants with other classmates during this strategy so they can share their knowledge base.

2. The teacher uses the rubric shown in Figure 3.2 for focused observation and evaluation. Again, the rubric can be used developmentally to track students' progress over the academic semester.

   • Students who consistently demonstrate the benchmark behavior are rated at the *Proficient* level. Students at this level are able to write the biography with ease and may even be advanced.

   • When students' behavior is inconsistent or mastery is not demonstrated, the teacher evaluates them as *Developing*. Students rated as *Developing* may be weaker in one component, but overall, their performance is acceptable.

- The final level, *Beginning,* describes students who rarely exhibit the benchmark behavior. Students evaluated as *Beginning* are not able to write the biography or are unable to perform several components of the rubric.

3. Teachers may give the rubric to students for self-assessment as they prepare to present their biographies to their peers.

Professional Resources to Explore

Camp, D. (2000). It takes two: Teaching with twin texts of fact and fiction. *Reading Teacher, 53,* 400–408.

Portalupi, J., & Fletcher, R. (2004). *In the beginning: Young writers develop independence.* Portland, ME: Stenhouse.

Tower, C. (2000). Questions that matter: Preparing elementary students for the inquiry process. *Reading Teacher, 53,* 410–423.

References

Antonacci, P., & O'Callaghan, C. (2004). *Portraits of literacy development: Instruction and assessment in a well-balanced literacy program, K–3.* Upper Saddle River, NJ: Merrill.

Armbruster, B., & Osborn, J. (2002). *Reading instruction and assessment.* Boston: Allyn & Bacon.

Braunger, J., & Lewis, J. P. (1997). *Building a knowledge base in reading.* Portland, OR: Northwest Regional Educational Laboratory.

Morrow, L. M., Pressley, M., Smith, J., & Smith, M. (1997). The effect of a literature based program integrated with literacy and science instruction with children from diverse backgrounds. *Reading Research Quarterly, 32*(1), 54–76.

Taylor, G. (2002). Who's who? Engaging biography study. *Reading Teacher, 56*(4), 342–344.

Tierney, R. J., & Shanahan, T. (1991). Research on the reading–writing relationship: Interactions, transactions, and outcomes. In R. Barr, M. L. Kamil, P. Mosenthal, & P. D. Pearson (Eds.), *Handbook of reading research* (Vol. 2, pp. 246–280). New York: Longman.

18 FAMILY HEROES

A Strategy for Developing Critical Thinking and Writing

INSTRUCTIONAL CONTEXT				
Grade Level	*Literacy Level*	*Group Size*	*Literature Genre*	*Literacy Skills*
● K–2	● Emergent	● Whole class	○ Fiction	● Comprehension
● 2–4	● Early	● 8–10 students	● Nonfiction	● Vocabulary
● 5–6	● Transitional	● 4–6 students		● Discussion
● 7–8	● Fluent	○ Individual		❖ Writing
				● Critical thinking

● Applicable	○ Not applicable	❖ Target skill

A Framework for Instruction

The Family Heroes strategy integrates critical thinking and the language arts and can be used across ages and grades. As students share their family stories, they are reading, writing, listening, and speaking for critical thinking (Antonacci & O'Callaghan, 2004). When oral language is integrated with literacy, students transfer knowledge gained in one domain into another (Morrow, Pressley, Smith, & Smith, 1997). The Family Heroes strategy helps students to grasp the style of expository text as they write factual texts about special members of their family.

As students develop the ability to write expository text, their reading comprehension of these formats also improves (Tierney & Shanahan, 1991). In addition, when reading and writing instruction are integrated, both areas improve more than when either domain is presented alone (Armbruster & Osborn, 2002; Braunger & Lewis, 1997). This section will illustrate how to implement this strategy across the curriculum as well as throughout the grades.

Learner Outcomes

- The students will write about family members who are or were heroes to others.
- The students will analyze their family heroes and define their character traits.
- The students will compare/contrast family heroes.

Instructional Procedure

The Family Heroes strategy is designed to help children investigate their own families histories and to discuss cultural differences. This strategy should be modeled by the teacher before students work on it independently.

Step by Step

1. The teacher begins by showing the class a picture of a family member who is or was a hero to others. "This is a picture of Aunt Mamie. I never met her, but I learned about her from my mother. My grandfather was a New York

95

FIGURE 3.3: Drawing of Family Hero

City police officer who died when my mother was six years old. At that time, in 1923, there were no pensions for widows, and my grandmother had no money to raise four children. Her sister, Aunt Mamie, was a school teacher who lived a very nice life of traveling and living alone. When my grandfather died, she moved in with my mother's family and used her salary to support the four children. Because of her sacrifice, all of the children went to college and led productive lives. To this day, when one member of the family helps another, we say, 'You are just like Mamie!'"

2. Each student discusses the topic with his or her parents or caregiver and selects one member of the family they regard as a hero. The student brings in a photo or may choose to create a drawing of his or her family member (see Figure 3.3). If a student is unable to identify a family hero, he or she may write about someone who is like a hero to him or her.

3. After selecting the family hero, each student writes what the person did that was heroic. The student also creates symbols to represent his or her family hero.

4. After the students have shared their family heroes, they can analyze their character traits. While students discuss their family heroes, they should listen for common traits.

5. After the students have defined the character traits for their own family heroes, they can meet in small groups of three to compare/contrast their heroes.

An Application of the Family Heroes Strategy for Grade 4

Mr. Sessay's fourth-grade class has been working on their writing skills all semester. The students are progressing but still struggle with writing factual

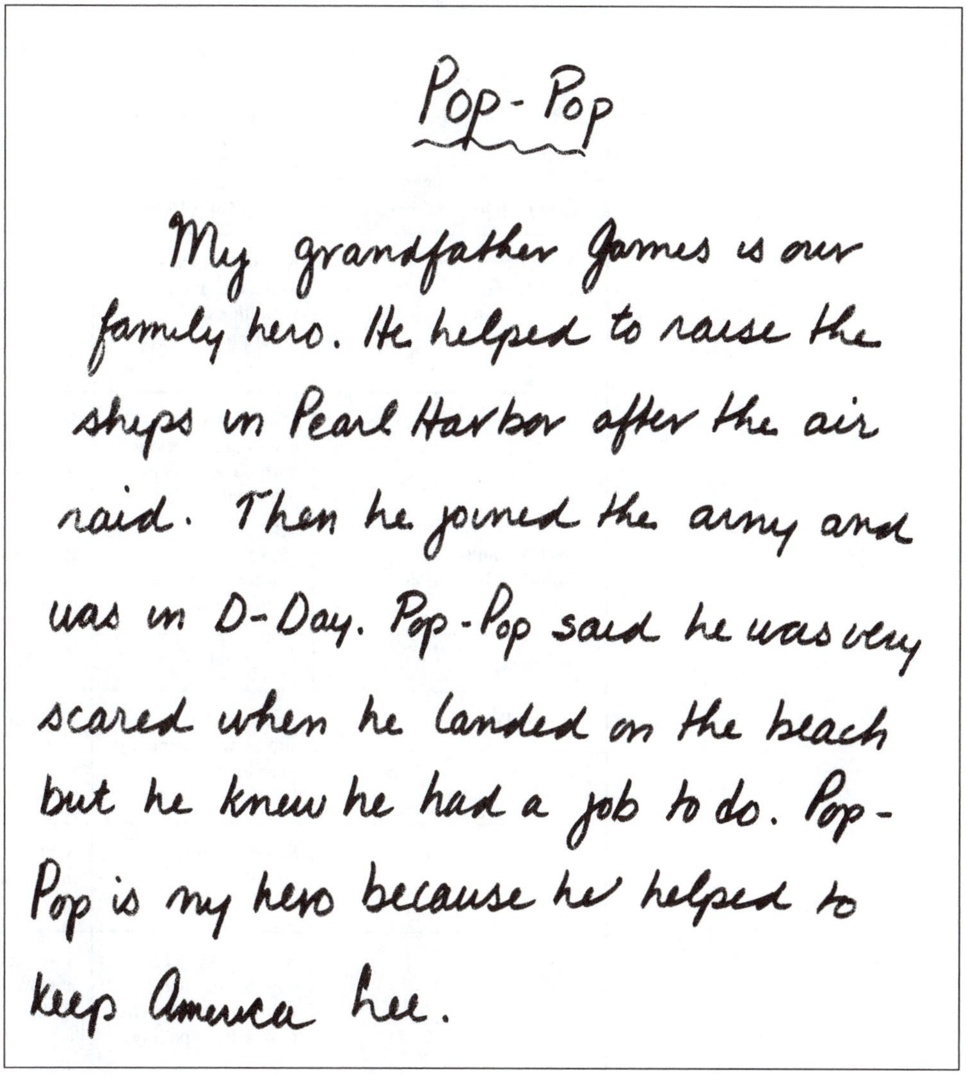

> ## Pop-Pop
>
> My grandfather James is our family hero. He helped to raise the ships in Pearl Harbor after the air raid. Then he joined the army and was in D-Day. Pop-Pop said he was very scared when he landed on the beach but he knew he had a job to do. Pop-Pop is my hero because he helped to keep America free.

FIGURE 3.4: Sample Biography of Family Hero

reports and essays. In order to help them improve their skills, Mr. Sessay has decided to implement the Family Heroes strategy that he learned about in last month's workshop. Each student has been given a graphic organizer and asked to discuss a family hero with a writing partner. James has chosen to write about his grandfather, James, who is a World War II veteran (see Figure 3.4).

After James shares his family hero story with Charlie, he presents it to his peers. When all of the students have presented their family hero stories, Mr. Sessay asks them if there are any traits that all the heros have in common. The students respond that the majority of family heroes were honest, brave, and hard working. Mr. Sessay has observed that even the struggling readers and writers are able to participate in this activity, and he is pleased with the students' progress.

Assessment Procedure

The purpose of the Rubric for Assessing Writing Biographies (Figure 3.5) is to guide the teacher in analyzing the students' family hero biographies.

Rubric for Assessing Writing Biographies

Name _____   Date _____

Story Elements	Beginning	Developing	Proficient
Main Character: Family Hero	Reference is made to main character with little or no description.	Main character is briefly described, with traits mentioned.	Main character is thoroughly described, clearly relating character traits to story events.
Story Events	One or two story events are mentioned with no relation to problem solution.	Some story events are mentioned; may be out of sequence.	Story events are clearly described with logical sequence.
Problem and Solution/Resolution	No solution or inaccurate problem is mentioned.	Problem is partially described or mentioned.	Problem is fully described and supported by details.
Writing	**Beginning**	**Developing**	**Proficient**
Vocabulary	Vocabulary is simple with some inaccuracies.	Some descriptive words are used. One or two words from book are used.	Vocabulary is rich and elaborate.
Sentence Structure	Sentence structure is simplistic with many errors.	Sentences may contain some grammatical errors.	Sentence structure is correct and elaborate.
Spelling	Many spelling errors appear; misspelled words are not aligned to standard spelling.	Some errors that are not close to standard spelling.	A few errors in spelling; misspelled words are closely aligned to standard spelling.
Punctuation	Many errors in periods and question marks. No attempt is made at using commas.	A few errors in use of periods and question marks. Some attempt is made at using commas.	Student rarely makes errors with punctuation.

FIGURE 3.5: Rubric for Assessing Writing Biographies

Step by Step

1. The teacher observes the students' literacy behaviors throughout the activity. English language learners might need extra support.

2. The teacher uses the rubric shown in Figure 3.5 for focused observation and evaluation. The rubric should be used over the course of a semester to note progress.

   • Students who consistently demonstrate the benchmark behavior are rated at the *Proficient* level. Students are rated as *Proficient* when they complete the family hero story with ease.

- When students' behavior is inconsistent or mastery is not demonstrated, the teacher evaluates the student as *Developing*. Students rated as *Developing* are weak in one or two components.
- The final level, *Beginning,* is given to students who rarely exhibit the benchmark behavior. Students rated as *Beginning* need a great deal of support to finish their family hero stories.

3. The teacher may give the rubric to students for self-assessment as they prepare to present their family stories to their peers.

Professional Resources to Explore

Atwell, N. (1987). *In the middle: Writing, reading, and learning with adolescents.* Portsmouth, NH: Heinemann.

Portalupi, J., & Fletcher, R. (2003). *Talking about writing.* Portland, ME: Stenhouse.

References

Antonacci, P., & O'Callaghan, C. (2004). *Portraits of literacy development: Instruction and assessment in a well-balanced literacy program, K–3.* Upper Saddle River, NJ: Merrill.

Armbruster, B. B., & Osborn, J. H. (2002). *Reading instruction and assessment: Understanding the IRA Standards.* Boston: Allyn & Bacon.

Braunger, J., & Lewis, J. P. (1997). *Building a knowledge base in reading.* Portland, OR: Northwest Regional Educational Laboratory.

Morrow, L. M., Pressley, M., Smith, J., & Smith, M. (1997). The effect of a literature based program integrated with literacy and science instruction with children from diverse backgrounds. *Reading Research Quarterly, 32*(1), 54–76.

Tierney, R. J., & Shanahan, T. (1991). Research on the reading–writing relationship: Interactions, transactions, and outcomes. In R. Barr, M. L. Kamil, P. Mosenthal, & P. D. Pearson (Eds.), *Handbook of reading research* (Vol. 2, pp. 246–280). New York: Longman.

A Strategy for Developing Writing Skills

INSTRUCTIONAL CONTEXT				
Grade Level	*Literacy Level*	*Group Size*	*Literature Genre*	*Literacy Skills*
● K–2	● Emergent	● Whole class	○ Fiction	● Comprehension
● 2–4	● Early	● 8–10 students	● Nonfiction	● Vocabulary
● 5–6	● Transitional	● 4–6 students		● Discussion
● 7–8	● Fluent	○ Individual		❖ Writing
				● Critical thinking

● *Applicable*	○ *Not applicable*	❖ *Target skill*

A Framework for Instruction

The Guided Writing strategy is a component of *Writer's Workshop* (see Figure 3.6), which is a period of time, usually at least one hour, for students to participate in a sustained writing session (Calkins, 1991 & 1994; Fountas & Pinnell, 2001). When students participate in Writer's Workshop, they are active in the subprocesses of writing, such as planning, composing, revising, editing, and publishing (Graves, 1983 & 1984).

During guided writing, the teacher acts as coach, meeting with groups of students who share certain needs, based on assessment data (Fountas & Pinnell, 2001). The teacher leads the students in an interactive lesson on a specific writing strategy that may focus on writing conventions or the craft of writing (Calkins, 1986 & 1994). For example, if the teacher observes that some students are having difficulty with paragraph structure, that would be the focus of the guided writing session. Atwell (1998) suggests that older students should keep writers' notebooks during mini-lessons and guided writing sessions, which become handy reference tools for them to use during independent writing.

Component	Description
Mini-lessons (15 minutes)	Using student work samples, the teacher focuses on: • a writing strategy • an aspect of grammar or spelling • topic selection through brainstorming
Guided writing (25 minutes)	The teacher may do one or more of the following: • Write with the class. • Hold individual conferences. • Hold group conferences.
Group share (20 minutes)	The teacher conducts a sharing session in which: • Students discuss their work. • Students discuss how they worked through the writing process.

FIGURE 3.6: Components of Writing Workshop

Learner Outcomes

- The students will engage in the writing process.
- The students will reflect on revision and their problems with composing text.
- The students will share their writing with peers.

Instructional Procedure

Guided writing facilitates the development of independent writing skills. Students gradually internalize the language of guided writing sessions, and this helps them become better editors of their own writing. This section will describe how to implement the strategy.

Step by Step

1. Based on assessment data, the teacher will gather a small group of four to five students to focus on a strategy or skill. The teacher may choose to group the students heterogeneously, as well.

2. The teacher will share with students a sample of student work with the name removed. For example:

> the man approached the house with fear. he looked at the
>
> broken windows with dread.

3. The teacher asks the group to study the sample and identify what has to be changed. The students respond that sentences must begin with capital letters.

4. Based on the students' responses, the group constructs a chart of rules regarding capitalization. For example:

> **CAPITALIZATION**
> 1. Sentences must begin with capital letters.
> 2. Proper nouns must begin with capital letters.
> 3. Places and names are proper nouns.

5. After the students have completed their texts, the teacher uses assessment data to determine if the group mastered the strategy or skill. The process is repeated, based on the data from this session.

An Application of the Guided Writing Strategy for Grade 1

During Thursday morning's literacy block period, the students in Ms. Besette's first-grade class are meeting on the carpet for guided writing. Ms. Besette has a sample of writing to show the small group of students and plans to ask them how they would edit the work. Here is the sample, which is based on H. A. Rey's (1941) book *Curious George:*

CURIOUS GEORGE

Curious George is just like me he always gets into trouble

my favorite part was when he ran away with the hat his

friend was very angry

After reading the writing sample, Ms. Besette asked the students what they would fix about the story response. Carl states that he would put in periods at the ends of sentences. Mikey mentions that the sentences also need to begin with capital letters. Ms. Besette reminds the students that last week they created a chart on capitalization, and she refers to it during this guided writing session. The students reread the rules for punctuation and promise to edit their stories for correct capitalization and punctuation.

Assessment Procedure

The purpose of the Rubric for the Writing Process (Figure 3.9) is to guide the teacher in analyzing students' work during the writing process. During the literacy block, the teacher writes anecdotal records to note students' participation and engagement. However, the rubric presented in this section can focus those observations on a specific writing task.

Step by Step

1. The teacher observes the students' literacy behaviors throughout the activity. The teacher may want to note if a given student struggled during the drafting stage before coming to the guided writing session.

2. The teacher uses the rubric shown in Figure 3.7 for focused observation and evaluation. The rubric may be used for the complete Writer's Workshop session, as it encompasses the drafting and editing phases.

   • Students who consistently demonstrate the benchmark behavior are rated at the *Proficient* level. This rating is for students who perform beyond grade level and are quick to edit their writing samples.

   • When students' behavior is inconsistent or mastery is not demonstrated, the teacher evaluates them as *Developing*. Students at this level are on grade level and may be advancing in one or two areas.

   • The final level, *Beginning*, is given to students who rarely exhibit the benchmark behavior. This rating is given to students who are unable to edit writing samples or who come to the session with incomplete work.

3. Teachers may give the rubric to students for self-assessment as they prepare to present their writing samples to their peers. It may also be used developmentally as an ongoing assessment instrument for an academic period.

Professional Resources to Explore

ERIC Clearinghouse on Elementary and Early Childhood Education
www.ericeece.org
The ERIC Clearinghouse offers teachers myriad activities as well as links to other sites across the curriculum.

Rubric for Assessing Students' Writing Development during Guided Writing

Name _____ Date _____

Writing Process	Beginning	Developing	Proficient
Planning	Student does not plan adequately for writing.	Student uses some reference tools and graphic organizers to plan text.	Student uses notebook, reference tools, and graphic organizers to plan text.
Composing	Student does not use planning to compose text.	Student uses some of planning process to compose text.	Student composes text based on planning and peer discussions.
Revising	Student does not revise text before publication.	Some text revisions are made based on conferences and strategy lessons.	Student revises text based on conferences and mini-lessons.
Editing	Student does not edit text before publication.	Student edits some errors from text.	Student edits text and deletes errors based on feedback and conferences.
Publishing	Student does not use care in preparing text for publication.	Text is somewhat ready for publication.	Student carefully prepares cover and text for publication.
Writing Skills	**Beginning**	**Developing**	**Proficient**
Vocabulary	Vocabulary is simple, with some inaccuracies.	Some descriptive words are used. One or two words from book are used.	Student uses descriptive words and vocabulary from notebook.
Sentence Structure	Sentence structure is incomplete.	Student somewhat uses reference tools and lessons to improve sentences.	Student uses strategy lessons and notebook to improve sentence structure.
Spelling	Many spelling errors; misspelled words are not aligned to standard spelling.	Words are close to standard spelling and student uses strategies to spell.	A few errors in spelling; misspelled words are closely aligned to standard spelling.
Punctuation	Many errors in periods and question marks. No attempt is made at using commas.	A few errors in use of periods and question marks. Some attempt at using commas is made.	Student revises and edits out errors in punctuation.

FIGURE 3.7: Rubric for the Writing Process

ERIC Clearinghouse on Assessment and Evaluation
http://ericae.net
This database offers teachers samples of assessment tools as well as links to other sites.

Calkins, L. M. (1994). *The art of teaching writing.* Portsmouth, NH: Heinemann.

Calkins, L. M. (1991). *Living between the lines.* Portsmouth, NH: Heinemann.

Dorn, L. J., & Soffos, C. (2003). *Developing independent learners: A reading/writing workshop approach.* Portland, ME: Stenhouse.

References

Atwell, N. (1998). *In the middle: New understandings about writing, reading and learning.* Portsmouth, NH: Heinemann.

Calkins, L. M. (1986). *The art of teaching writing* (2nd ed.) Portsmouth, NH: Heinemann.

Calkins, L. M. (1991). *Living between the lines.* Portsmouth, NH: Heinemann.

Calkins, L. M. (1994). *The art of teaching writing.* Portsmouth, NH: Heinemann.

Fountas, I. C., & Pinnell, G. S. (2001). *Guiding readers and writers, grades 3–6.* Portsmouth, NH: Heinemann.

Graves, D. H. (1983). *Writers: Teachers and children at work.* Portsmouth, NH: Heinemann.

Graves, D. H. (1994). *A fresh look at writing.* Portsmouth, NH: Heinemann.

Children's Literature Reference

Rey, H. A. (1941). *Curious George.* New York: Houghton.

A Strategy for Developing Literacy through Oral Language

INSTRUCTIONAL CONTEXT				
Grade Level	Literacy Level	Group Size	Literature Genre	Literacy Skills
● K–2	● Emergent	● Whole class	● Fiction	● Comprehension
● 2–4	● Early	● 8–10 students	● Nonfiction	● Vocabulary
● 5–6	● Transitional	● 4–6 students		● Discussion
○ 7–8	○ Fluent	● Individual		❖ Writing
				● Critical thinking

● Applicable	○ Not applicable	❖ Target skill

A Framework for Instruction

The Language Experience Story strategy uses the students' oral language to develop literacy skills (Stauffer, 1970). The students share an experience, such as a field trip or holiday, and dictate their text to the teacher, who acts as scribe (Ashton-Warner, 1965). Talking together and sharing experiences is an essential way of exploring ideas, researching problems, and enhancing literacy (Smith, 2001). After the students have talked about their experiences and the teacher has dictated the story, the text becomes the reading material for instruction. The value of using the students' own language for reading text is that they are intrinsically motivated to read about their adventures. The text can also be used for extension activities, such as sentence builders and vocabulary lessons.

English language learners also benefit from the Language Experience Story strategy, as it allows them to hear language while observing its phonology (Drucker, 2003). The interactive reading of text also provides opportunities for shared reading, which will increase fluency. The active engagement during the activity, as well as the interaction of oral language and literacy, makes the Language Experience Story strategy important for the primary grades and English-as-a-second-language (ESL) instruction. The rationale for this strategy can be summarized as follows:

- What I can think about, I can talk about.
- What I can say, I can write.
- What I can write, I can read.
- I can read what I write and what other people write for me to read (Van Allen & Halvoren, as cited in Drucker, 2003, p. 26).

Learner Outcomes

- The students will discuss a common experience or story.
- The students will dictate their text to the teacher.
- The students will read the text.

Instructional Procedure

The Language Experience Story strategy integrates reading, writing, listening, and speaking. It is a versatile strategy and may be used to summarize stories students have read or to report on factual experiences. This section will provide directions to implement this strategy.

Step by Step

1. After a field trip or other common experience, the teacher guides the students in a discussion using a few questions. For example, before Halloween, the teacher might ask, "Who would like to tell us about his or her costume?"

2. When the children have finished discussing the topic, the teacher asks them to begin dictating the text. For example, the teacher might create the following chart, based on the students' dictation:

HALLOWEEN

We are excited about Halloween. Our costumes are ready for our party. John is going to be a pirate. Isabel is pretending to be a ballerina. Jennifer is dressing up as a queen. We can hardly wait to carve our pumpkin into a jack-o-lantern.

---

3. As the teacher is writing the text, the children can be asked to come up and write the first letter of a word or to provide the punctuation at the end of a sentence. The teacher can focus on skills that the students need to develop, based on the assessment data.

4. After the text has been written, the students read the chart as a choral reading of text. The teacher may call on individual children to come up and read specific sentences or to circle key vocabulary words.

5. Several extension activities can be done to follow up the language experience approach, such as creating a picture dictionary based on students' text or making a pocket chart of vocabulary words. A picture dictionary is an excellent strategy for English language learners (see Figure 3.8).

An Application of the Language Experience Story Strategy for Grade 1

It is February in Ms. Wahl's first-grade classroom. The students are eager to talk about their trip to the Shore Wildlife Center, where the park ranger showed them the natural habitats of several animals. Ms. Wahl opens up the discussion by asking the students to talk about their favorite experiences during the field trip. Several students mention picking up the huge horseshoe crabs, while others talk about the jellyfish in the large tank. After discussing the trip, Ms. Wahl asks the students to summarize their trip for their *First-Grade Book of Memories*, which they have kept since September. The class writes about special events through the language experience approach, and in June, they will display their book for their parents and friends from other classes. Here is the entry for the trip to the wildlife center:

OUR TRIP TO THE SHORE WILDLIFE CENTER

We went to the beach on February 9 to visit the Wildlife Center. We had a good time and the park ranger took us on a nature walk. We saw horseshoe crabs, jelly fish, clams and sandpiper birds. We saw a chart of ocean life and how pollution hurts ocean life. It was very cold but we had fun.

Jj

jack o lantern

I love to make a

jack o lantern!

FIGURE 3.8: Sample Page from Picture Dictionary

Assessment Procedure

The purpose of the Rubric for Assessing Language Experience Stories (Figure 3.9) is to guide the teacher in analyzing the students' story. The rubric can be modified to evaluate language experience stories that are retellings of fictional texts.

Step by Step

1. The teacher observes the students' literacy behaviors throughout the activity. The teacher should note whether all students participate in the discussion before dictation. This discussion is a critical prewriting step and helps students to construct an adequate knowledge base for reading and writing.

2. The teacher uses the rubric shown in Figure 3.9 for focused observation and evaluation. The rubric may be modified to fit the needs of the students or the particular event.

   - Students who consistently demonstrate the benchmark behavior are rated at the *Proficient* level. Students are rated as *Proficient* when their performance is advanced or beyond the minimum requirements.
   - When students' behavior is inconsistent or mastery is not demonstrated, the teacher evaluates them as *Developing*. Performance is rated as *Developing* when students are on target in most areas.

Rubric for Assessing Language Experience Stories

Name _____   Date _____

Story Elements	Beginning	Developing	Proficient
Story Events	One or two story events are mentioned with sequence.	Some story events are mentioned but may be out of sequence.	Story events are clearly described with logical outline.
Details/Elaboration	No event is described. Vocabulary and sentence structure are very poor.	Event is partially described and has some details. Student uses grade-level vocabulary and sentence structure.	Event is fully described and supported by details. Student uses rich vocabulary and elaborate sentence structure.
Oral Story	Student is unable to generate oral story.	Student partially generates story but needs some prompting.	Student is able to generate story orally for dictation.

SUMMARY OF PERFORMANCE

FIGURE 3.9: Rubric for Assessing Language Experience Stories

- The final level, *Beginning,* is given to students who rarely exhibit the benchmark behavior. When students are unable to participate in the discussion or language experience dictation component, they are rated as *Beginning.*

Professional Resources to Explore

The Kids.com
www.thekids.com
This site has illustrated stories from around the world.

National Association for the Education of Young Children
www.naeyc.org
This early childhood website offers myriad activities and lesson plans for the preschool and primary-grade teacher.

Beales, D., de Temple, J., & Dickinson, D. (1994). Talking and listening that support literacy development of children from low-income families. In D. Dickinson (Ed.), *Bridges to literacy: Children, families and schools.* Cambridge, England: University of Cambridge Press.

Daniels, H., & Bizer, M. (2004). *Teaching the best practice way*. Portland, ME: Stenhouse.

References

Ashton-Warner, S. (1965). *Teacher*. New York: Simon & Schuster.

Drucker, M. J. (2003). What reading teachers should know about ESL learners. *Reading Teacher, 57*(1), 22–29.

Smith, P. G. (2001). *Talking classrooms: Shaping children's learning through oral language instruction*. Newark, DE: International Reading Association.

Stauffer, R. G. (1970). *The language experience approach to the teaching of reading*. New York: Harper & Row.

A Strategy for Developing Writing of Expository Texts

INSTRUCTIONAL CONTEXT				
Grade Level	*Literacy Level*	*Group Size*	*Literature Genre*	*Literacy Skills*
● K–2	● Emergent	● Whole class	● Fiction	● Comprehension
● 2–4	● Early	● 8–10 students	● Nonfiction	● Vocabulary
● 5–6	● Transitional	● 4–6 students		● Discussion
● 7–8	● Fluent	● Individual		❖ Writing
				● Critical thinking

● Applicable	○ Not applicable	❖ Target skill

A Framework for Instruction

The Learning Journal strategy provides teachers with multiple opportunities to integrate the language arts across the curriculum. Students use learning journals to construct meaning from the textbooks or reference materials they read. As students respond to the textbooks they are reading, they are conducting an *internal conversation,* which helps them to understand the concepts as well as content (Britton, 1970).

The process of *journaling* helps students construct the meanings of difficult concepts and vocabulary (Bromley, 1993). This *writing-across-the-curriculum* activity is critical to accessing and expanding students' existing knowledge bases (Walmsley & Walp, 1990). Even young children can benefit from journal writing, as it helps them to transfer their knowledge from one domain to another (Morrow, Pressley, Smith, & Smith, 1997). The Procedure section describes how to include learning journals in your classroom.

Learner Outcomes

- The students will summarize and analyze text in their journals.
- The students will activate prior knowledge and interpret the content of what they read.
- The students will explore the topic or reading through their journal entries.

Instructional Procedure

There are many different types of journal activities. This strategy focuses on *learning journals*. However, the Application section will describe how to implement other types of journaling experiences.

Step by Step

1. Before students read their textbook or literary selection, the teacher prepares them by activating their prior knowledge through a graphic organizer.

> Journal Entry for Chapter 20
> Page 123
>
> President Kennedy was elected in 1960. He was from a large family in Massachusetts. During WWII he was hurt in a boat accident. I want to find out how the accident happened.

FIGURE 3.10: Sample Learning Journal Entry

2. After the students have filled in the concepts they already know about the topic, they record their questions regarding the topic. For example:
   • What did President Kennedy do while he was president?
   • Why did he create the space program?
   • Why was he killed?

3. After the students have finished recording their questions, they can begin to read the selection. The teachers may suggest that students use stick-on notes to record any questions that develop as they read the selection.

4. The teacher may choose to have students stop at key sections in the chapter to respond in their learning journals or to read to the end of the chapter. An example of a learning journal entry is shown in Figure 3.10.

5. The students should record vocabulary words they do not understand or questions they still have about the text in their learning journals. After they have finished the chapter, the teacher can revisit the graphic organizer and the students can add new concepts to it (see Figure 3.11).

6. The students should refer to their journals to check that all of their questions regarding the topic have been answered. If they have not answered their questions, the students can begin research projects to explore the topic further.

An Application of the Learning Journals Strategy for Grade 4

Teachers can utilize several different types of journals in the classroom. *Double-entry journals* provide students with explicit practice in interpreting text. In this type of journal, students write their responses to the text. Double-entry

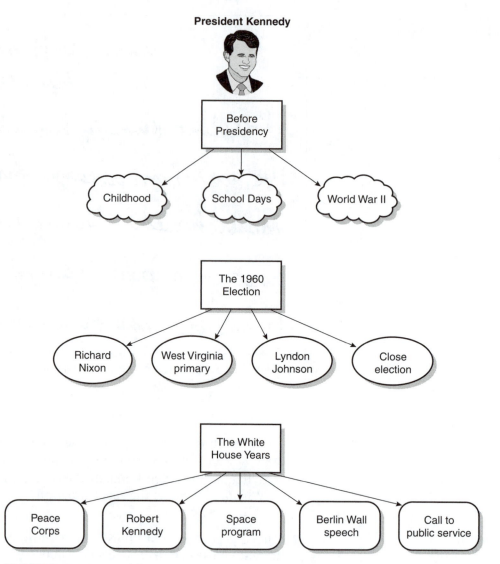

FIGURE 3.11: Sample Graphic Organizer for after Reading

journals can be used with both narrative and expository text structures. Figure 3.12 is an example of an entry by a fourth-grader.

Simulated journals are primarily used with literature study. As students read a book or story, they select a character and write a journal entry from that perspective. In order to write an entry as a certain character, the student must use

TEXT EXCERPT	REACTION/RESPONSE TO TEXT
During the Battle of Long Island, about 1,500 of George Washington's troops were killed or injured. Washington himself was in danger of being captured, but he discovered the plot and escaped to New Jersey.	I wonder how Washington was able to escape without the British finding out.

FIGURE 3.12: Sample of Double-Entry Journal

> *Molly's Journal*
>
> *August 1776*
>
> *Hello my name is Molly. I am ten years old and live in Brooklyn by the river. Last night there was a big battle with the red coats. I am very scared. Father said we may have to leave our farm.*

FIGURE 3.13: Sample Entry from a Simulated Journal

critical thinking to interpret events through another's perspective and to write in that voice. The excerpt shown in Figure 3.13 is an example of a simulated journal entry.

Assessment Procedure

The purpose of the Annotated Checklist for Journal Writing (Figure 3.14) is to help teachers gather data to inform instruction about students' conceptual understanding. The checklist can be modified to include double-entry or simulated journals.

Step by Step

1. The teacher observes the students during the learning journal activity and focuses on certain students. During the course of one month, every student should be evaluated.

Annotated Checklist for Journal Writing

Name _____   Date _____

Observable Behaviors	O	NO	NA
Summarizes content and interprets it.			
Raises questions and lists difficult vocabulary words.			
Integrates prior knowledge of topic with new knowledge.			
Participates in class discussions about journal entries.			
Chooses challenging topics to explore.			
Maintains focus in journal entries.			

OBSERVATION NOTES AND COMMENTS

LEGEND:
O: Observed
NO: Not Observed
NA: Not Applicable

FIGURE 3.14: Annotated Checklist for Journal Writing

2. The teacher uses the checklist to focus his or her observations. If a student displays the benchmark behavior, the "O" box is checked. If the behavior is not demonstrated, then the "No" box is checked.

3. The checklist should be used periodically to assess the students' development over the academic year. Students may also use the checklist for self-assessment.

Professional Resources to Explore

National Council of Teachers of English (NCTE)
www.ncte.org
The National Council of Teachers of English offers teachers many links to integrate literacy across the content areas.

Burkhardt, R. M. (2002). *Writing for real: Strategies for engaging adolescent writers.* Portland, ME: Stenhouse.

Routman, R. (1994). *Invitations: Changes as teachers and learners, K–12.* Portsmouth, NH: Heinemann.

References

Britton, J. (1970). *Language and learning.* Harmondsworth, England: Penguin.

Bromley, K. (1993). *Journaling: Engagements in reading, writing, and thinking.* New York: Scholastic.

Morrow, L. M., Pressley, M., Smith, J., & Smith, M. (1997). The effect of a literature based program integrated with literacy and science instruction with children from diverse backgrounds. *Reading Research Quarterly, 32*(1), 54–76.

Walmsley, S. A., & Walp, T. P. (1990). Integrating literature and composing into the language arts curriculum, philosophy and practice. *Elementary School Journal, 90*(3), 251–274.

A Strategy for Developing Writing Fluency for Social Interaction

INSTRUCTIONAL CONTEXT				
Grade Level	**Literacy Level**	**Group Size**	**Literature Genre**	**Literacy Skills**
● K–1	● Emergent	● Whole class	● Fiction	● Comprehension
● 2–4	● Early	● 8–10 students	○ Nonfiction	● Vocabulary
● 5–6	● Transitional	● 4–6 students		● Discussion
● 7–8	● Fluent	● Individual		❖ Writing
				● Critical thinking

● Applicable	○ Not applicable	❖ Target skill

A Framework for Instruction

The Message Board strategy provides a natural approach for encouraging students to interact with others through written messages and sketches or drawings. *Message boards* have a variety of possibilities for different grade levels. In the primary grades, children may write simple notes to one another and post them on the message board, or they may select pen pals from the upper grades or another school and write letters to them. Students in the upper grades may use e-mail with students in other schools across the country. Chat rooms are especially useful for groups of students engaging in online discussion when it is tied to a research project in which students are searching for information on the same topic. When this is the case, the function of language changes from *social interaction* to *heuristic,* the function of language that is used for learning.

Why encourage students to use message boards? There are many purposes for using language. Halliday (1975) describes language as *functional* and identifies seven purposes or functions of language, both written and spoken. One function of language is social interaction, or *interactional language,* which is used to create and maintain relationships with others. Within the classroom context, interactional language is not emphasized and is given little practice in the literacy curriculum. When students do not practice one or more of the language functions, they fail to develop skills and strategies in those areas. Therefore, teachers who create a classroom context that provides for the use of interactional language will help students develop the communication skills necessary for social interaction.

Learner Outcomes

- Students will use language for social interaction on a regular basis.
- Students will become frequent users of the message board, thereby facilitating writing fluency.

Instructional Procedure

Step by Step

1. The teacher prepares a large bulletin board and designates it as the "Message Board." The bulletin board should be one to which the students have easy access, so they can reach it, and one that is at their eye level. Since there will be a great deal of activity around the message board, it should be located in an out-of-the-way area of the classroom so that the activity will not pose an interruption.

2. The teacher and students arrange all of their names on the message board. Print each student's first name on an envelope, and then fasten it to the message board:

   The envelopes may be made from oak tag, durable enough to withstand putting in and taking out messages.

3. The teacher works with students to compose a set of rules and procedures for using the message board. The teacher leads the students in a discussion to determine their expectations for using the message board as well as the procedures for posting and collecting messages. The students should be part of writing the rules for using the message board.

4. The teacher demonstrates how the message board may be used. Children may need time to learn to write messages and understand why messages are written. For younger students, as well as some older students, the teacher may find it useful to model writing messages.

5. Set aside a time for posting and reading messages for efficient classroom management. For example, the teacher may consider a time in the morning for students to post messages and a designated time after lunch for reading messages.

6. Teachers in the middle grades should consider e-mail for older students and electronic message boards. Although many students use e-mail with their friends, the teacher may set up a system of pen pals with classrooms of children from other schools across the nation.

7. The teachers may encourage students who are at the emergent stage of writing to draw pictures and write labels. The students may then have the opportunity to talk with the students to whom they have written to explain their messages.

An Application of the Message Board Strategy for Grade 1

Mr. Parker, a first-grade teacher, decided to use the Message Board strategy in his class. His purpose was to engage students in authentic writing to develop writing fluency and, at the same time, to provide them with an opportunity to write for personal communication and social interaction. Mr. Parker used a bulletin board that was in the children's reach, decorated it with a seasonal theme, and placed an envelope with each child's name on the message board. He explained how to write a message, and he and the students wrote rules for using the class message board. The next day, all of the students found messages from

Mr. Parker carefully placed in their oak tag envelopes, which were attached to the message board.

One of the rules the class created was that if you receive a message, then you should answer it. (This rule answers the question that is often posed by the student who does not receive a message!) The time after lunch was set aside for the students to write messages to their friends. After getting messages from their teacher, they were exuberant and couldn't wait to begin to write their first letter and then their second, third, and fourth. They were so excited in writing and receiving messages from their friends that Mr. Parker found it difficult to take them away from writing to transition to the next lesson.

The next morning, the students came into the room and immediately went to the message board to deliver the letters they had written at night. And it was not assigned homework! Figure 3.15 shows Stella's message to Joy. Stella is at the transitional stage of literacy development.

Assessment Procedure

One of the purposes of the Message Board strategy is to provide students with the opportunity to write for social interaction and personal communication. Another purpose is to develop students' fluency in writing. Therefore, students who write often will develop writing fluency. In assessing students' use of the message board, teachers will evaluate the frequency that students engage in writing and how they use the message board. Although the content of the message will not be assessed, the teacher may wish to determine whether the messages sent by the students can be read by the recipients.

Dear Joy,
I am having. a partey at my hous. Can you com? We will hav fun. Ask your mom.
Love Stella

FIGURE 3.15: Stella's Message to Joy

Step by Step

1. The teacher observes the students during the time allocated for message board writing. During this time, students write messages and read those they have received. The teacher carefully observes one or two students to assess and document their frequency in writing.

2. The teacher uses the form in Figure 3.16 to document his or her observations of students' writing of messages. The teacher writes the date of the observation and, next to each skill, notes whether the student was observed performing it. The following code may be used to record the skills that were observed:
   - *O:* The teacher observed the student using a particular literacy behavior.
   - *NO:* The teacher did not observe the student using a particular literacy behavior.
   - *NA:* The particular literacy behavior did not apply.

Assessment Checklist for Using Message Boards

Name _____ Grade _____ School Year _____

Concepts and Skills	Date	Date	Date	Date	Date	Date	Date
Frequently uses message board.							
Writes messages to many students.							
Enjoys writing and receiving messages.							
Follows classroom rules and procedures for using message board.							
Writes messages that have purpose.							
Writes messages that can be understood by readers.							
Comments							

O: Observed
NO: Not Observed
NA: Not Applicable

FIGURE 3.16: Assessment Checklist for Using Message Boards

Professional Resources to Explore

ERIC Clearinghouse on Languages and Linguistics Digest
www.cal.org/ericcll/digest/ncrcds.04html
This website offers resources on facilitating second-language development in children.

Berrill, D. P., & Gall, M. (2000). *Penpal programs: In the primary classroom.* Portland, ME: Stenhouse.

Hennings, D. (2001). *Communication in action.* Boston: Allyn & Bacon.

References

Halliday, M. A. K. (1975). *Learning how to mean: Explorations in the function of language.* London, England: Edward Arnold.

A Strategy for Developing Writing Skills in Young Children

INSTRUCTIONAL CONTEXT				
Grade Level	*Literacy Level*	*Group Size*	*Literature Genre*	*Literacy Skills*
● K–1	● Emergent	● Whole class	● Fiction	● Comprehension
● 2–4	● Early	● 8–10 students	● Nonfiction	● Vocabulary
○ 5–6	● Transitional	● 4–6 students		● Discussion
○ 7–8	● Fluent	○ Individual		❖ Writing
				● Critical thinking

● *Applicable*	○ *Not applicable*	❖ *Target skill*

A Framework for Instruction

The Shared Pen strategy uses an interactive approach in teaching writing to young students. The strategy is designed like the language experience approach, where students dictate their stories to the teacher. Using the Shared Pen strategy, the teacher and students write a story together while learning about the conventions of print. At first, the teacher acts as a scribe as the group composes text. As the children learn more about writing, the teacher invites them to "share the pen": "How do we spell that word? Take the pen and write the word."

By sharing the pen with the children in composing text, the teacher "guides their participation" in writing, offering young writers a scaffold for learning about the conventions of print (Rogoff, 1990). Through this interactive writing strategy, children can take risks to produce more challenging texts, knowing that they will receive the necessary support from their guide. The teacher will model and demonstrate how to compose the text, which will be read by the class during shared reading. The reading-and-writing connection is apparent during the Shared Pen strategy: Children are learning more about reading through shared writing, a literacy learning principle supported by Clay (1991), who emphasizes that learning to write means learning more about reading. For the literacy curriculum in the primary grades, shared or interactive writing plays an important part in balancing the program.

Learner Outcomes

- The students will participate with the teacher in composing the text, offering ideas and sentences for the story.
- The students will participate in using correct conventions of language in writing.

Instructional Procedure

The Shared Pen strategy sustains the participation of each group member, as students focus on learning a writing skill. Therefore, whatever topic is selected for writing, it should be a shared group experience that promotes active involvement by all group members. For example, after the children in a first-grade classroom took a field trip to the zoo, they wrote a group story on what they observed. Typically, fiction and nonfiction stories, lists, large story maps, "wall stories," and directions to follow in class are some examples of group writing appropriate for the Shared Pen strategy. The stories are written on large pieces of paper and displayed for class readings.

Step by Step

1. The teacher secures a large sheet of chart paper to the easel. The paper should be placed at the students' level, so they can read and write on it.

2. Beginning with a teacher-led discussion, the teacher prepares the students by helping them to focus on ideas for writing about a topic. Included in the discussion are the following: the purpose for writing, ideas that may be part of the story, and how to begin the story.

3. The teacher begins writing the story with the students. Throughout the writing, the teacher includes meaningful talk about the story, commenting on interesting words to use, helping children to rework awkward sentences, and showing children how to build stories by connecting sentences in a logical sequence. Routman (2000) suggests that teachers use the following prompts during a shared writing lesson:
   - Who has a good beginning sentence?
   - How else can we say that? How about if we say it this way?
   - How can we combine those two thoughts?
   - Who has another idea?
   - What do you think about . . . ?
   - Is there anything else you think we should include here?
   - Where do you think we should add that? (p. 39)

4. The teacher takes opportunities to conduct mini-lessons throughout the writing process. *Mini-lessons* are short lessons on specific writing skills, such as the use of capital letters or punctuation marks, or they may be used to help students organize their sentences to make sense to their audience.

5. After writing each sentence, the teacher directs the children to reread the text to include the previous sentence, "testing it out" to demonstrate to the children that it should make sense.

6. At the conclusion of the writing, the teacher encourages the students to read their story all the way through, from the beginning to the end, "to see if it makes sense."

An Application of Shared Writing for Grade 2

Linda Baker's second-grade class was involved with a science experiment: They were hatching ducks. The students were responsible for turning the eggs three times a day. They were to take turns turning the eggs, and they knew they had to be careful handling the eggs. After Linda had a discussion on the procedure, the class decided to write the instructions to be followed by each student who turned the eggs. Using the Shared Pen approach, Linda and the students wrote "Instructions for Turning Duck Eggs."

Assessment Procedure

Kidwatching is a term coined by Yetta Goodman to describe observation as a process that teachers use to assess and document children's growth in language and literacy. Observing students' literacy behaviors occurs during instruction.

However, without recording what they have observed, teachers will forget the literacy growth students make and the areas for improvement for which teachers must plan.

1. During the Shared Pen activity, the teacher focuses on one child, observing and recording his or her writing behaviors.

2. The teacher uses the form in Figure 3.17, attached to a clipboard, to record the child's writing behaviors.

3. When the session is over, the teacher may add any comments on the child's areas of strengths or needs for improvement.

Professional Resources to Explore

Clay, M. M. (1975). *What did I write? Beginning writing behaviour.* Portsmouth, NH: Heinemann.

Fletcher, R., & Portalupi, J. (1998). *Craft lessons: Teaching writing K–8.* Portland, ME: Stenhouse.

Portalupi, J., & Fletcher, R. (2001). *Nonfiction craft lessons: Teaching information writing K–8.* Portland, ME: Stenhouse.

McCarrier, A., Pinnell, G. S., & Fountas, I. C. (2000). *Interactive writing: How language and literacy come together, K–2.* Portsmouth, NH: Heinemann.

References

Clay, M. (1991). *Becoming literate: The construction of inner control.* Portsmouth, NH: Heinemann.

Rogoff, B. (1990). *Apprenticeship in thinking: Cognitive development in social context.* New York: Oxford University Press.

Routman, R. (2000). *Conversations: Strategies for teaching, learning, and evaluating.* Portsmouth, NH: Heinemann.

Observation Checklist for Shared Pen

Name _____ Grade _____ School Year _____

Concepts and Skills	Date	Date	Date	Date	Date	Date	Date
Engages in prewriting story discussion.							
Suggests ideas for story.							
Offers sentence to represent ideas.							
Knows where to start writing story.							
Suggests spellings of words.							
Knows to use a capital letter to begin sentence.							
Suggests period to end sentence.							
Suggests question mark to end sentence.							
Writes a letter.							
Writes a word.							
Reads story back.							
Responds with necessary changes.							
(If the child was able to write a letter or word without a prompt, record each in the box under the date.)							
Comments							

Code for Using the Observation Checklist:
O: Observed
NO: Not Observed
NA: Not Applicable

FIGURE 3.17: Observation Checklist for Shared Pen

A Strategy for Encouraging Creative Story Writing

INSTRUCTIONAL CONTEXT				
Grade Level	*Literacy Level*	*Group Size*	*Literature Genre*	*Literacy Skills*
○ K–1	○ Emergent	● Whole class	● Fiction	● Comprehension
● 2–4	○ Early	● 8–10 students	● Nonfiction	● Vocabulary
● 5–6	● Transitional	● 4–6 students		● Discussion
● 7–8	● Fluent	● Individual		❖ Writing
				● Critical thinking

● *Applicable*	○ *Not applicable*	❖ *Target skill*

A Framework for Instruction

The Story Impressions strategy is a prereading activity, with a focus on the creative construction of writing stories through the use of key words selected from a story. Prior to reading a story, the students make predictions about it using teacher-selected key words or phrases from the story. Using the key words, students write their first impressions of the story. After reading the story, students then write summaries of it, comparing them with their first impressions.

Developed by McGinley and Denner (1987), the Story Impressions strategy provides students with the opportunity to create a first draft of a story even before they read it. The strategy is designed around making predictions from clues. *Predicting* is a very powerful reading strategy that helps students to understand text (McNeil, 1984). When students make predictions while they read, they must activate their prior knowledge, thereby making deeper connections to the text and deriving greater meaning from the story. The Story Impression strategy makes use of predictions to have students construct their own stories. Denner and McGinley (1987) found that as a prereading/writing activity, the Story Impressions strategy had positive effects on the comprehension of narrative text by students in grades 2 through 8.

The clues that the students use are key words from the original story, either single words or phrases. Working in small groups, students brainstorm how the key words can be used to construct a story that may be close to the one they will read. Students then read the book and compare the author's story with theirs in a postreading activity.

The Story Impressions strategy has been used with fiction and nonfiction texts. When the strategy is applied to narrative literature, students benefit in several ways:

1. Students' prior knowledge about story content and narrative structure of text is activated and brought into play, as they construct a story around key words.

2. Students learn about the key vocabulary words through a meaningful discussion prior to reading and working to construct a story around the key words.

3. At the conclusion of their reading, the students engage in text connections by comparing their texts to the author's text.

When applying the strategy to content-area disciplines, there are comparable benefits related to student learning:

1. Students' prediscussion of key words encourages them to activate their prior knowledge and to increase their understanding of the critical concepts to be learned.

2. Students' use of prior knowledge in developing written impressions of the concept to be read heightens their awareness of what they may *know* and what they need to *learn* related to what they will read.

3. When students engage in a postreading discussion and compare their initial impressions with the text material, they think deeper about the concepts they are learning.

There are many ways to adapt the Story Impressions strategy for the needs of different students:

1. For English language learners, the key words may be presented with pictures accompanied by a more elaborate discussion of the concepts and vocabulary.

2. Students who are not fluent writers may dictate their first impressions of the story to the teacher, who acts as a scribe. This first story impression written down by the teacher serves as a model to the student, who may need help in getting started.

3. For students with special needs who have difficulty writing longer stories, the teacher may direct them to write one sentence to tell about the beginning of the story, one sentence to describe the middle, and one to explain how the story will end.

Learner Outcomes

- The students will engage in a discussion of key words and phrases related to their assigned readings.
- The students will write story impressions using selected key words or phrases from the story.
- The students will compare two texts, the author's with their own story impressions, to determine congruency.

Instructional Procedure

The implementation of the Story Impressions strategy will differ as it is applied to various grades and literacy levels and for different types of texts that are selected for reading (e.g., narrative stories or expository informational text). For example, for students in the first and second grades who are not fluent readers and writers, the teacher will provide greater support during the prediscussion and will engage in interactive writing, where the students and teacher compose the story and the teacher writes the story on large sheets of chart paper. Appropriate support is also given to students in the middle grades who are struggling readers and writers. Demonstrating how to use key words by writing together will offer students the needed assistance. For students who are English language learners, the use of pictures during the discussion of key words is a needed scaffold that will help them in their writing.

Step by Step

1. The teacher previews the text to select key words and phrases related to the development of the story plot and other important information in the text. Depending on the length of the book and the grade level of the students, the teacher decides on the appropriate number of key words and phrases, which is from ten to twenty. The teacher may choose single words or two- or three-word phrases that are of significance to building the story or text.

2. The teacher arranges the key words in the order that students will encounter them in their reading.

3. The teacher prepares the key words on a graphic organizer, such as in Figure 3.18. The key words also may be listed on a worksheet, on the chalkboard, on an overhead transparency, or on a large sheet of chart paper.

4. The teacher introduces the story or the text to the students. The teacher engages the students in an introduction of the assigned reading to motivate them and to activate their prior knowledge.

5. The teacher presents the key words to the students, who may be working in small groups. The purpose of the prediscussion is to brainstorm the meanings of the words and their connections to the overall story or information. If a narrative text will be read, the key words will relate to the story's parts. The students will make predictions of the story problem using the key words as clues. If an informational text will be read, the key words will relate to concepts or content. The students will make predictions about the content or the information they will read using the key words as clues.

6. The teacher directs the students to write their own stories of their impressions of the book. If the students are working with an expository text, they will draft their impressions about the content or information in the text.

7. After students complete their story impressions or their drafts of the content of the text, the teacher directs them to read the actual text. As students read, they compare the author's story with theirs. If the students are reading an expository text, they compare their draft impressions with the information in the text.

8. The teacher conducts a postreading discussion, where students compare their story impressions. Students reading a narrative text discuss their different story impressions and how their stories compare to the author's. There is no one correct story impression. Students reading an informational text discuss the differences between their drafts in terms of content and how it is explained in the text, making necessary adjustments to their draft impressions to correct the information.

9. To extend this strategy for reading a narrative text, students may be given another set of key words to develop their own stories. For students reading an informational text, they may revise their drafts so that they contain the correct information.

An Application of the Story Impressions Strategy for Grade 5

The Story Impressions strategy was used with a group of fifth-graders who were studying the Irish potato famine. After the students had read *Nory Ryan's Song,*

FIGURE 3.18: Graphic Organizer for Story Impressions

by Patricia Reilly Giff (2000), the teacher used the Story Impressions strategy for reading the sequel to the book, *Maggie's Door* (2003). The students knew about the setting of the book and used the key words to write their first impressions of the story. After they read *Maggie's Door*, they wrote summaries of the book, their second story impressions, and compared them with their first story impressions. See Figure 3.19, which shows a sixth-grader's story impressions of *Maggie's Door*.

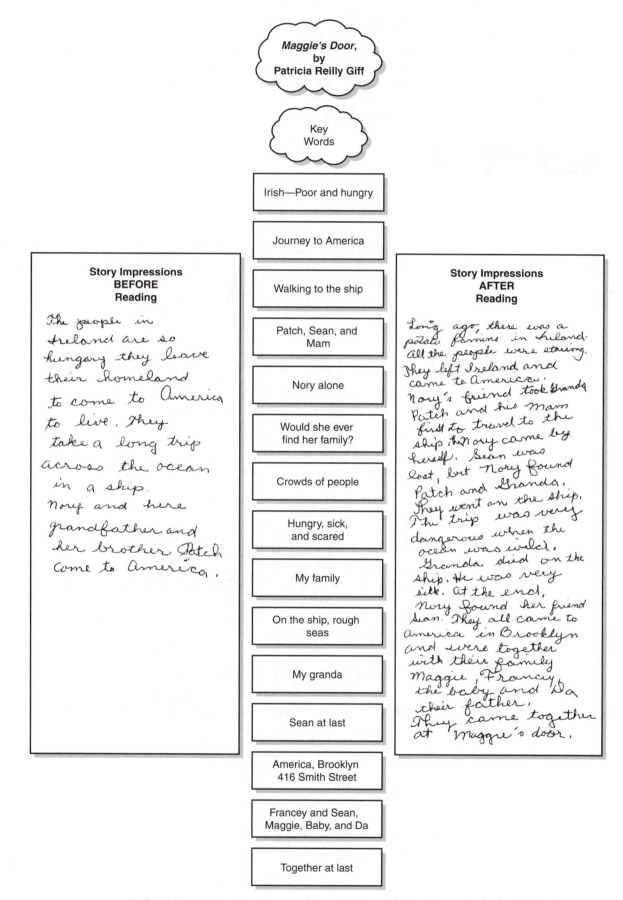

Maggie's Door,
by
Patricia Reilly Giff

Key
Words

Irish—Poor and hungry

Journey to America

Walking to the ship

Patch, Sean, and Mam

Nory alone

Would she ever find her family?

Crowds of people

Hungry, sick, and scared

My family

On the ship, rough seas

My granda

Sean at last

America, Brooklyn 416 Smith Street

Francey and Sean, Maggie, Baby, and Da

Together at last

Story Impressions BEFORE Reading

The people in Ireland are so hungary they leave their homeland to come to America to live. They take a long trip across the ocean in a ship. Nory and here grandfather and her brother Patch come to America.

Story Impressions AFTER Reading

Long ago, there was a potato famine in Ireland. All the people were staring. They left Ireland and came to America. Nory's friend took Granda Patch and his Mam first to travel to the ship. Nory came by herself. Sean was lost, but Nory found Patch and Granda. They went on the ship. The trip was very dangerous when the ocean was wild. Granda died on the ship. He was very sick. At the end, Nory found her friend Sean. They all came to America in Brooklyn and were together with their family Maggie, Francey the baby and Da their father. They came together at Maggie's door.

FIGURE 3.19: Story Impressions of *Maggie's Door* by a Sixth-Grade Student

Assessment Procedure

Teachers will want to determine how students have met these learning outcomes: (1) students' active participation in pre- and postreading discussions, (2) their use of prior knowledge in discussions and in their written stories or text impressions, and (3) their writing skills. A rubric for evaluating these skills is provided in Figure 3.20.

Step by Step

1. The teacher observes the students during the discussion of the words. He or she rates their participation and use of prior knowledge during the discussion.

2. The teacher collects the written stories for evaluation. The pre- and postreading stories are evaluated for understanding of concepts, reading comprehension, vocabulary use, sentence structure, and mechanics of language. After assessing the story impressions, the teacher uses the codes provided to document the student's level of proficiency for each of the writing skills.

Professional Resources to Explore

Buehl, D. (2001). *Classroom strategies for interactive learning* (2nd ed.). Newark, DE: International Reading Association.

Buss, K., & Karnowski, L. (2000). *Reading and writing literary genres.* Newark, DE: International Reading Association.

Norton, T., & Land, B. L. J. (2004). *Literacy strategies: Resources for beginning teachers, 1–6.* Upper Saddle River, NJ: Merrill/Prentice Hall.

References

Denner, P. R., & McGinley, W. (1986). The effects of story-impressions as a pre-reading/writing activity on story comprehension. *Journal of Education Research, 82*(6), 320–326.

McGinley, W., & Denner, P. (1987). Story impressions: A pre-reading/writing activity. *Journal of Reading, 31*, 248–253.

McNeil, J. (1984). *Reading comprehension: New directions for classroom practice.* Glenview, IL: Scott, Foresman.

Children's Literature References

Giff, P. R. (2003). *Maggie's door.* New York: Wendy Lamb.

Giff, P. R. (2000). *Nory Ryan's song.* New York: Dell Yearling.

Annotated Checklist for Assessing Story Impressions

Name _____   Date _____

Book Title _____   Author _____

Discussion Skills	B	D	P
1. Actively participates in discussion.			
2. Uses prior knowledge to construct meanings of key words.			
3. Demonstrates discussion skills: turn taking, listening skills, voice modulation, and articulation.			

COMMENTS ON DISCUSSION SKILLS

Written Story	B	D	P
1. Constructs a complete story based on key words.			
2. Demonstrates prior knowledge in story development.			
3. Demonstrates understanding of the story.			
4. Contains vocabulary consistent with student's literacy level.			
5. Contains sentence structure consistent with student's literacy level.			
6. Contains spelling consistent with student's literacy level.			
7. Contains punctuation and capital letters consistent with student's literacy level.			

COMMENTS ON WRITING SKILLS

Codes:

Beginning (B): Student is beginning to develop the skill and needs much assistance from the teacher. Many errors are apparent.

Developing (D): Student is developing the skill and needs little assistance from the teacher. Few errors are apparent.

Proficient (P): Student shows a strong development of the skill and needs no assistance from the teacher. No errors are apparent.

FIGURE 3.20: Annotated Checklist for Assessing Story Impressions

A Strategy for Developing Writing through Written Story Retelling and Note Taking

INSTRUCTIONAL CONTEXT				
Grade Level	*Literacy Level*	*Group Size*	*Literature Genre*	*Literacy Skills*
○ K–1	○ Emergent	● Whole class	● Fiction	● Comprehension
● 2–4	● Early	● 8–10 students	● Nonfiction	● Vocabulary
● 5–6	● Transitional	● 4–6 students		● Discussion
● 7–8	● Fluent	● Individual		❖ Writing
				● Critical thinking

● *Applicable*	○ *Not applicable*	❖ *Target skill*

A Framework for Instruction

The Written Story Retelling and Note Taking strategy involves the retelling of a story that students have heard or read by writing the parts of the story that they remember. As an adjunct to students' recalling and organizing the parts of the story for written retellings, note taking has been added through the use of story mapping. Students may be encouraged to add pictures to their written retellings to further elaborate on them. Although this strategy focuses on the written retelling of a story, there are many formats for story retellings—oral retellings, story illustrations, storytelling, and dramatic renditions of a story (Brown & Cambourne, 1987; Morrow, 1985).

Often, story retelling is classified as an assessment strategy and its instructional value is largely overlooked. The benefit of written retelling to students is that they deepen their story comprehension because they must think more intensely about what they have read and order the parts in a logical sequence (Brown & Cambourne, 1987; Koskinen, Gambrell, Kapinus, & Heathington, 1988).

Most students at the transitional and fluent literacy levels have a competency in writing that allows them to write more and to write faster. Therefore, it would seem that written retellings would be appropriate for most students at these stages of literacy development, although early and emergent readers and writers may indeed participate in written story retellings. In any case, not all students, even those at the fluent stages of literacy development, are competent in organizing the story elements in their written retellings. This is especially true for children who have little or no experience with story retellings. Benson and Cummins (2000) call for a developmental approach to introducing written story retellings that is similar to the writing process. Such an approach will permit children to prepare for their written retellings by thinking through what they will write.

Learning Outcomes

- The students will read or listen to a story and use story maps to take notes.
- The students will use their notes to construct complete written retellings of the story that include the story elements and their own personal responses.

Instructional Procedure

The Written Story Retelling and Note Taking strategy will be especially helpful to students who find writing difficult, especially those with little or no skill in organizing what they have read or heard. These students do not know where to begin in retelling a story. For English language learners, the story map serves as a visual representation of the story, which they may use in recalling the most important parts.

Step by Step

1. The teacher prepares for the written story retellings by selecting the book that the children will read and then analyzing it into its basic story parts.

2. Using a form like the one in Figure 3.21, the teacher develops a Story Retelling Guide to serve as a scoring key for assessing children's written retellings.

<table>
<tr><td colspan="2" align="center">**Story Retelling Guide**</td></tr>
<tr><td>**Story Elements**</td><td align="center">**Literature**</td></tr>
<tr><td>Title</td><td>*Lon Po Po: A Red-Riding Hood Story from China*</td></tr>
<tr><td>Author</td><td>Ed Young</td></tr>
<tr><td>Characters</td><td>The three children: Shang, Tao, and Paotze; the wolf; the children's mother</td></tr>
<tr><td>Setting</td><td>The home of the children in the countryside of northern China</td></tr>
<tr><td>Problem</td><td>The wolf disguised as the children's granny, Po Po, tried to trick the children so that he could come in and eat them.</td></tr>
<tr><td>Story Events Initiating Event</td><td>• When the children were left alone by their mother, who went to visit their grandmother on her birthday, a wolf in disguise tricked his way into the house.</td></tr>
<tr><td>Story Events Leading to the Solution</td><td>• The wolf was dressed like the children's grandmother and said that he was sick and wanted to come into the house.
• The children let the wolf come into the house.
• Shang finally discovered that the wolf was not their Po Po when she felt its tail and its claws and saw its face in the candlelight.
• Shang, the eldest child, decided to trick Lon Po Po, *"Granny wolf,"* by tempting it with gingko nuts. She told the wolf that they were sweet, delicious, and magic.
• Shang made up a plan and told her two sisters.
• The three girls would climb to the top of the gingko tree and persuade the wolf to come up to eat the nuts.
• They let down a basket for Lon Po Po to climb in and then to be lifted to the top of the tree.</td></tr>
<tr><td>Story Solution</td><td>• Each time they lifted the wolf a little higher, they dropped him to the bottom of the tree until he was lifted to the very top and dropped. This allowed Shang, Tao, and Paotze to escape into their house, where they locked the door until their mother returned.</td></tr>
<tr><td>Personal Response</td><td>Each student response differs.</td></tr>
</table>

FIGURE 3.21: Story Retelling Guide for *Lon Po Po: A Red-Riding Hood Story from China*

3. The teacher prepares the students for note taking by teaching them how to use the As-You-Read Story Map, shown in Figure 3.22. The following is a sample set of instructions that the teacher may use with students to help them use the story map for taking notes:

  a. Distribute story maps to the students. Tell them that using the map while they are reading the story will assist them in organizing the story parts before they write their story retellings.

  b. Discuss the map with the students, reviewing the story parts and demonstrating how to use the map during reading to take notes about the story. An effective modeling approach is the *think-aloud*. That is, read a portion of the book and think out loud about how to summarize what you have read. Show the students the steps in the summarization of story parts. Finally, write the summary of ideas on the story map.

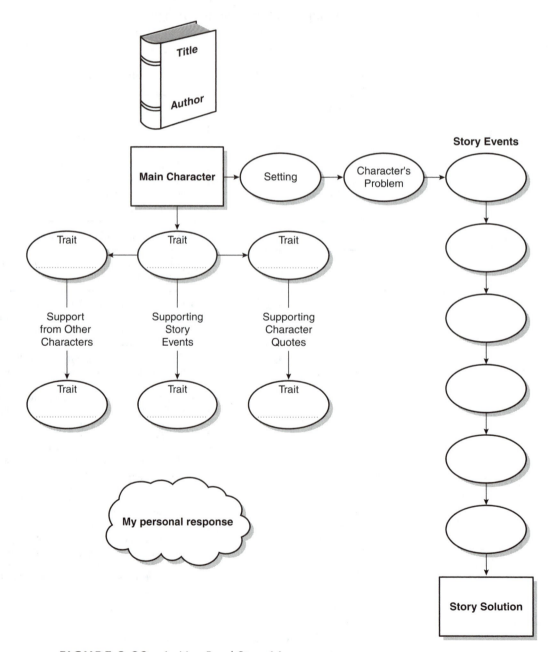

FIGURE 3.22: As-You-Read Story Map

c. When students experience problems in remembering the story parts, the teacher may use these cue questions to prompt them for the elements:

QUESTIONS FOR CUEING STORY ELEMENTS

Character: Who was in the story? Who was the story about?

Setting: Where did the story take place? When did it happen?

Beginning of the Story: What happened at the very beginning of the story?

Middle of the Story: What happened next? Then what happened? What did _____ do next?

End of the Story: How did the story end? How was the problem solved?

Response to the Story: Tell why you did or didn't like the story? What did you learn from the story? Why do you think the author wrote the story?

---

4. The teacher prepares the children for reading the selected piece of literature by conducting a book introduction. This includes discussing the title and the cover illustration to help children make predictions about the story.

5. After the students finish reading the story, they use the story map to take notes and organize their ideas before writing their retellings. The teacher directs them to retell the story by writing down what they can remember and using their notes on the story map to help them.

6. The students then use their notes to compose their written story retellings.

An Application of Written Story Retellings with Note Taking for Grade 3

The students in the third grade were preparing to read and take notes through story mapping and then to use their maps to retell the story in written format. Their teacher prepared for the instructional sequence by developing a retelling guide for the book that the students would read, as shown in Figure 3.21. After a thorough book introduction, the students read the story and the teacher gave them the As-You-Read Story Map, shown in Figure 3.22. The teacher guided the students in using their notes to write their story retellings. When they finished, the students shared their written retellings in small groups. The teacher used the assessment rubric for written story retellings (Figure 3.23) to evaluate the students' competencies in retelling a story using a written format.

Assessment Procedure

The teacher uses the Rubric for Assessing Written Story Retelling, shown in Figure 3.23, as a guide in analyzing the student's written retelling as well as the Story Retelling Guide that she developed (Figure 3.21). This is a holistic method of assessment. Therefore, the teacher looks for patterns of student proficiencies in literacy concepts and skills as well as areas that need improvement.

Step by Step

1. After students complete their written story retellings, the teacher assesses each student's written story retelling.

Rubric for Assessing Written Story Retellings

Story Elements	Inadequate	Developing	Proficient
Main Character	Reference is made to main character with little or no description.	Main character is briefly described, with traits mentioned.	Main character is thoroughly described and character traits are clearly related to story events.
Story Problem	No reference is made to story problem.	Story problem is mentioned.	Thorough description of story problem is made.
Story Events	One or two story events are mentioned with no relation to problem solution.	Some story events are mentioned. May be out of sequence.	Story events are clearly described and sequenced accurately. Relation of story events to problem is clearly made.
Problem Solution/Resolution	No problem solution is mentioned or part of problem is briefly mentioned.	Problem is briefly described or mentioned.	Problem is fully described and supported by details that relate to story elements.
Personal Reaction	No brief reaction is made but lacks personal connection.	Brief response with personal connection is present.	Thoughtful, well-developed response with several personal connections is present.
Writing	**Inadequate**	**Developing**	**Proficient**
Presentation of Ideas	Ideas do not follow story structure; writing lacks coherence.	Ideas are presented with some degree of coherence.	Ideas are presented logically and with coherence that follows story structure.
Vocabulary	Vocabulary is simple, with some inaccuracies.	Some descriptive words are used. One or two words from book are used.	Vocabulary is rich and variety of words are used; accuracy in word usage is evident.
Sentence Structure	Sentence fragments and run-on sentences appear in writing.	A few run-on sentences and fragments are present.	No sentence fragments or run-on sentences.
Spelling	Many spelling errors, making it difficult to read; misspelled words are not aligned to standard spelling.	Some spelling errors; misspelled words do not interfere with understanding of story and some are aligned to standard spelling.	Few or no errors in spelling; the misspelled words are closely aligned to standard spelling.
Punctuation and Capital Letters	Many errors in periods and question marks. No attempt is made at using commas.	A few errors in use of periods and question marks. Some attempt at using commas is made.	Writing demonstrates understanding of use of quotation marks, periods, question marks, commas, etc.

FIGURE 3.23: Rubric for Assessing Written Story Retellings

2. For assessing the story content and organization, the teacher uses the Story Retelling Guide and follows this procedure:
   a. Use the story guide to determine the accuracy of the story content and organization.
   b. Additionally, use the rubric as a guide to determine the level of proficiency that the student reached—Proficient, Developing, or Beginning—in describing each story part.

3. To assess the student's writing, the teacher uses the second part of the Rubric for Assessing Written Story Retellings, which is marked "Writing" (see Figure 3.27). Assess the student's writing for vocabulary, spelling, sentence structure, and punctuation. Use the rubric as a guide to determine the level of proficiency that the student has reached.

Professional Resources to Explore

Benson, V., & Cummins, C. (2000). *The power of retelling: Developmental steps for building comprehension.* Bothell, WA: Wright Group.

Morrow, L. M. (1985). Retelling stories: A strategy for improving young children's comprehension, concept of story structure, and oral language. *Elementary School Journal, 85*(5), 647–661.

References

Benson, V., & Cummins, C. (2000). *The power of retelling: Developmental steps for building comprehension.* Bothell, WA: Wright Group.

Brown, H., & Cambourne, B. (1987). *Read and retell: A strategy for the whole-language/natural learning classroom.* Portsmouth, NH: Heinemann.

Koskinen, P. S., Gambrell, L. B., Kapinus, B. A., & Heathington, B. S. (1988). Retelling: A strategy for enhancing students' reading comprehension. *Reading Teacher 41*(9), 892–896.

Morrow, L. M. (1985). Reading and retelling stories: Strategies for emergent readers. *Reading Teacher, 41*(9), 892–896.

Children's Literature References

Young, E. (1989). *Lon Po Po: A Red-Riding Hood story from China.* New York: Scholastic.

Instructional and Assessment Strategies for Developing DISCUSSION SKILLS

Within this section are strategies to help students develop their discussion skills. Although the emphasis is on strategies in oral language presentations, students will be involved in using other forms of language to complete each activity.

A Strategy for Facilitating Personal, Text, and World Connections

INSTRUCTIONAL CONTEXT				
Grade Level	*Literacy Level*	*Group Size*	*Literature Genre*	*Literacy Skills*
● K–1	● Emergent	● Whole class	● Fiction	● Comprehension
● 2–4	● Early	● 8–10 students	● Nonfiction	● Vocabulary
● 5–6	● Transitional	● 4–6 students		❖ Discussion
● 7–8	● Fluent	○ Individual		● Writing
				● Critical thinking

● *Applicable*	○ *Not applicable*	❖ *Target skill*

A Framework for Instruction

The Connect It! strategy emphasizes the construction of meaning through teacher-led discussions before, during, and after reading. Text discussions are intended to help students make connections to the text. Strategic readers use this very powerful tool to create meaning from the text (Harvey & Goudvis, 2000). Readers connect to the story in three different ways:

1. They make *personal connections,* or text-to-self connections, relating something that happened in the story to their own experiences.

2. They make *text connections,* or text-to-text connections, relating two different aspects within the same text or connecting the text they are reading with a different book they have read.

3. They make *world connections,* or text-to-world connections, relating something that happened in the text to an event that occurred in the world around them. Figure 4.1 provides a brief definition and an example of each of the three types of text connections. Once students have learned how to connect with text, it is expected that they will internalize this strategy, thereby connecting to their readings without the intervention of the teacher.

Learner Outcomes

- Students will participate in prereading and postreading discussions.
- Students will make text-to-self connections.
- Students will make text-to-text connections.
- Students will make text-to-world connections.

Instructional Procedure

The Connect It! strategy consists of three phases: the prereading discussion phase, the reading phase, and the postreading discussion phase. During the discussion phases of the strategy, the teacher facilitates the students in making connections with the book through guiding questions.

Defining Text Connections		
Text-to-Self Connections	**Text-to-Text Connections**	**Text-to-World Connections**
In this type of connection, readers connect their personal experiences and their own lives to what they read in the text or they connect background knowledge to the concepts in the text.	When readers are engaged in text-to-text connections, they relate the events in one text to those that they have read in another. They may also connect the themes, the characters, the plots, the literary style, etc. from two or more texts.	Text-to-world connections are made when readers connect events in the story to world events.

Examples of Text Connections		
Text-to-Self Connections	**Text-to-Text Connections**	**Text-to-World Connections**
In reading Paula Danziger's book *Amber Brown Goes Fourth,* Tanya made a personal connection when she responded during a discussion about how she felt the same way as Amber when she moved last year and how she lost her two friends, Annie and Lizzie.	When children read *Yeh-Shen: A Cinderella Story from China,* they compared all of the elements of this version to those in *The Talking Eggs,* the French Creole version. This is a text-to-text connection because children look at similarities and differences between the stories.	In the story by Eleanor Clymer, *The Trolley Car Family,* the Parker family must make their home in a trolley car because the father loses his job when trolley cars are replaced. Two examples of making world connections with this book are to the issue of homelessness as well as the loss of a job as a result of changes made by inventions.

FIGURE 4.1: Types of Text Connections
Source: Based on Antonacci & O'Callaghan, 2004, p. 279.

Step by Step

The Prereading Discussion Phase

1. The teacher introduces the book to the students to help them begin to make connections to the story. Depending on the story, the teacher introduces the students to an event or the main character and asks them to make connections. The teacher facilitates the process by using guiding questions that help students make specific kinds of connections. If the students have problems making different kinds of connections, the teacher should model each type of connection for them.

2. The teacher distributes and introduces to the students the graphic organizer, Figure 4.2, Connect It! See My Connections. He or she takes as much time as the students need to help them understand what the graphic represents.

3. As the book introduction and discussion proceed, the teacher encourages the students to make personal connections and share them with the group. After sharing, they use the graphic organizer to record their personal connections. The teacher continues to lead the discussion, helping students make book or text connections and world connections, and invites them to share their connections with the group and record them on the graphic organizer.

The Reading Phase

1. The teacher provides time for students to read and directs them to continue to make different types of connections with the text as they read. The teacher

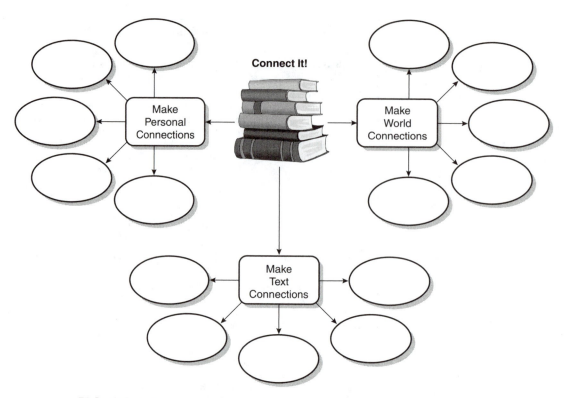

FIGURE 4.2: Connect It! See My Connections

encourages the students to think about the story while they are reading to make connections.

2. The teacher encourages the students to put themselves in the story and to reflect on similar personal events (personal connections); to think of how different parts of the story relate or how other stories they have read are the same or different (text connections); and finally, to identify something in the story that is the same as an event that took place in their neighborhood, their community, or the world (world connections).

3. The students continue to record their connections on their graphic organizers.

The Postreading Discussion Phase

1. The teacher offers an opportunity for students to share the connections they made while reading and encourages them to continue to make connections during the story discussion.

2. After the students have finished reading, they engage in a postreading discussion, in which the teacher invites the students to share their connections. The teacher may extend the discussion through the use of questions to facilitate students to think more deeply about the story and to help them make more connections.

This strategy may be used at all levels. However, for the emergent and early literacy level, the teacher should model text connections and ask students to make connections using the discussion format. For students with special needs, direct instruction in making text connections is critical in their developing comprehension strategies. The teacher begins by teaching one type of text connection at a time. During independent reading and reading aloud, it is important to remind students to connect to the story, using a short review.

An Application of the Connect It! Strategy to Grade 3

A third-grade group of students identified as having special needs is learning about folk tales. They have read different versions of traditional folktales. They began their study by reading different versions of the folktale "The Mitten." After reading two versions of this folktale, one by author Jan Brett (1989) and one by author Yevonne Pollock (1986), the teacher began to teach the students how to connect different aspects of the stories. They discussed the aspects of the two stories that were the same and different. The teacher and the children made a group chart that compared the animals and the main characters from the two different versions of "The Mitten." The students learned how to make text-to-text connections.

Assessment Procedure

During the pre- and the postdiscussion phases of the strategy, the teacher observes the students with respect to their level of participation and the types of connections that they are making. The students are also asked to think about their own performances with respect to the three phases: pre- and postdiscussion and reading.

Step by Step

1. The teacher observes each student during the pre- and postdiscussion phases of the strategy. The teacher should note the kinds of connections the student makes during the discussion. To determine if the student is making the kinds of text connections during the reading phase, the teacher will listen to his or her contributions during postreading discussion. The teacher can determine from the discussion whether the student was making the connections during the reading phase. The teacher may use the student's graphic organizer to examine the connections he or she made during the reading phase.

2. The teacher engages students in a self-assessment of their discussion and reading performances with respect to the types of text connections made. Provide copies of the self-assessment form shown in Figure 4.3 to the students and guide them through the directions. A student's self-assessment of his or her participation in the discussions and his or her reading performance is important in developing the positive practice of making text connections during independent reading.

3. After the students have assessed themselves, the teacher collects their rating scales and records his or her own evaluations of their discussion and reading performances.

Professional Resources to Explore

Harvey, S. (2002). Nonfiction inquiry: Using real reading and writing to explore the world. *Language Arts, 80*(1), 12–22.

Stead, T. (2002). *Is that a fact? Teaching non-fiction writing, K–3.* Portland, ME: Stenhouse.

Strickland, D. S., Ganske, K., &. Monroe, J. (2002). *Supporting struggling readers and writers: Strategies for classroom intervention, 3–6.* Portland, ME: Stenhouse.

References

Antonacci, P. A., & O'Callaghan, C. M. (2004). *Portraits of literacy development: Instruction and assessment in a well-balanced literacy program, K–3.* Upper Saddle River, NJ: Merrill/Prentice Hall.

Harvey, S., & Goudvis, A. (2000). *Strategies that work: Teaching comprehension to enhance understanding.* York, ME: Stenhouse.

Student and Teacher Rating Scale for Making Connections during Reading

Student Name _____   Date _____

Book Read _____

Directions: Please rate your performances for participating in the discussions and for making connections to your reading. Follow the rating scale for each question.

Poor Performance   Great Performance

1 ——————————————————————————————— 10

Discussions: Pre- and Postdiscussions	Student	Teacher
Did I honestly participate in the prereading and postreading discussion?		
Did I make text-to-self connections during the discussion?		
Did I make text-to-text connections during the discussion?		
Did I make text-to-world connections during the discussion?		
Reading the Book		
Did I set a purpose for reading?		
Did I make text-to-self connections during the discussion?		
Did I make text-to-text connections during the discussion?		
Did I make text-to-world connections during the discussion?		

COMMENTS: STUDENT

COMMENTS: TEACHER

FIGURE 4.3: Rating Scale for Making Connections during Reading

Children's Literature References

Brett, J. (1989). *The mitten.* New York: Putnam's.
Clymer, E. (1947). *The trolley car family.* New York: Scholastic.
Danziger, P. (1995). *Amber Brown goes fourth.* New York: Putnam.
Louie, A. (1982). *Yeh-Shen: A Cinderella story from China.* New York: Philomel.
Pollock, Y. (1986). *The old man's mitten.* New York: Scholastic.
San Souci, R. D. (1989). *The talking eggs.* New York: Dial.

A Strategy for Promoting Understanding through Talk

INSTRUCTIONAL CONTEXT				
Grade Level	*Literacy Level*	*Group Size*	*Literature Genre*	*Literacy Skills*
○ K–1	○ Emergent	● Whole class	● Fiction	● Comprehension
○ 2–4	○ Early	● 8–10 students	● Nonfiction	● Vocabulary
● 5–6	● Transitional	● 2–6 students		❖ Discussion
● 7–8	● Fluent	○ Individual		● Writing
				● Critical thinking

● *Applicable*	○ *Not applicable*	❖ *Target skill*

A Framework for Instruction

The Discussion Web strategy (Alvermann, 1991) structures classroom talk so that students focus their conversations on issues related to their reading. Students engage in instructional conversations that help clarify their thinking about ideas, activate prior knowledge before reading, and set their own purposes for reading a text. They use graphic organizers that assist in structuring the discussion and in recording the major ideas from their discussions, as shown in Figure 4.5. Students work in small groups of two and then in larger groups to come to a consensus on differing points of view. The process students follow that is associated with the dialogue is represented in Figure 4.4.

The three phases of the Discussion Web strategy lead to students' engagement in literate thinking around an instructional topic:

- *Phase 1:* Students are prepared to read the text through a student-led discussion that helps them to set a purpose for reading and activate their prior knowledge.

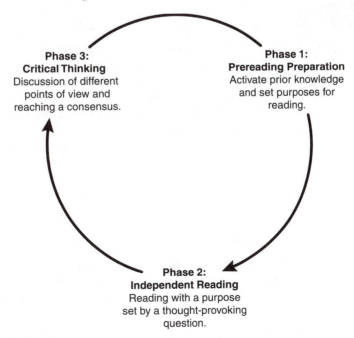

Phase 3:
Critical Thinking
Discussion of different points of view and reaching a consensus.

Phase 1:
Prereading Preparation
Activate prior knowledge and set purposes for reading.

Phase 2:
Independent Reading
Reading with a purpose set by a thought-provoking question.

FIGURE 4.4: Discussion Web Sequence

- *Phase 2:* Students engage in reading, asking questions related to the text.
- *Phase 3:* Students use their readings to enter into a discussion that leads to position statements.

Many educators and researchers place a premium on classroom talk and dialogic inquiry because such discussions lead students to the construction of meaning around the topic and to higher levels of thinking. This type of classroom talk differs from traditional teacher-led discussions, which are centered on teacher-initiated questions followed by student responses. Wells (2001) makes a case for dialogic inquiry in learning: "The mediating role of dialogue in knowledge building is probably most evident in face-to-face discussion, where one speaker immediately responds to another" (p. 186). *Dialogic inquiry* is characterized by a discussion among students who are seeking real answers to questions. Such classroom talk is described by Cazden (1988) as "real discussion . . . in which ideas are explored rather than answers to teachers' test questions provided and evaluated" (p. 54).

Learner Outcomes

- Students will participate in a prereading discussion.
- Students will read with a purpose.
- Students will participate in small-group discussion, voicing their ideas about the instructional topic.
- Students will listen to other points of view and reach a consensus regarding the question.
- Students will share their opinions with the class.

Instructional Procedure

The major parts to the Discussion Web strategy are (a) preparing the students for reading, (b) reading of the text by the students, (c) using the discussion web graphic in small-group discussions to structure student talk, and (d) reaching consensus by group members and sharing points of view among class members.

Step by Step

1. The teacher prepares the students to read by initiating a thorough discussion that (a) activates their prior knowledge, (b) helps them set a purpose for reading, and (c) introduces new vocabulary to them.
   a. Introduce the book and help activate students' prior knowledge by encouraging them to make connections with the content or the issue through common experiences.
   b. During the discussion, encourage students to set a purpose for reading. For example, having students make predictions about what they will read will help them read for a purpose. Similarly, hearing part of the text may make students want to read it to find out how it unfolds or to learn more about the content.
   c. The prereading discussion will also include some critical vocabulary words that will help readers understand the text.

2. The teacher then introduces the students to the discussion web. After students have read or listened to the story, demonstrate to them how the discussion web works. Give them copies of a web similar to the one in Figure 4.5, which was used by one teacher (as discussed later in the Application section).

3. The teacher divides the students into pairs, presents them with a debatable question related to the text, and has each group discuss both sides of the

question. As they come up with reasons, they should record each one with key words in the appropriate column on the chart, "Yes" or "No." The students then reach a conclusion based on their arguments.

4. After pairing the students, the teacher encourages them to engage in a small-group discussion to further the inquiry. Combine two pairs of students into a small group of four. Have students look at their reasons in the "Yes" and "No" columns, along with their conclusions. Encourage each group to come to a consensus based on the supporting statements. To reach agreement, it is often necessary for some students to give up their points of view. Because this may be difficult, Alvermann (1991) suggests that the teacher needs to encourage students to keep an open mind, reminding them that they will have an opportunity to voice their opinions during the large-group discussion.

5. The teacher directs the students to come together for a whole-class discussion. During this aspect of the strategy, each small group selects one member to share his or her consensus on how the group reached an agreement. It is at this point that members who had strong disagreements with the group may voice their conclusions, providing a set of arguments to support their opinions.

6. The teacher may provide follow-up activities to extend students' understanding. When students complete extension activities, they will explore the issues surrounding the discussion even further. For example, writing persuasive essays will give them the opportunity to articulate the arguments to support their conclusions.

An Application of the Discussion Web for Grade 7

The seventh-graders in Harry Johnson's science class were in the middle of a unit on the physical effects of tobacco on the human systems. Part of the unit included interviewing adults in their families who started to smoke when they were young to learn about what got them started. Mr. Johnson presented two articles—one from a local newspaper and one from a national magazine—on different views related to the impact of advertising on getting young people to smoke. After reading the articles, the teacher paired the students for a discussion of the two points of view. To guide students' instructional conversations, Mr. Johnson prepared the graphic organizer found in Figure 4.5.

Assessment Procedure

Assessing students' participation in the Discussion Web strategy is achieved through the students' self-assessment followed by their teacher's evaluation of their discussion skills. The teacher first encourages the students to think about their own performances using the questions on the rating scale. Following the students' self-assessment, the teacher evaluates their performances and compares the two ratings. A follow-up conference with each student is used to focus on his or her strengths, areas for improvement, and discrepancies between the two assessments.

Step by Step

1. The teacher observes the students during the discussion to assess them on their discussion skills.

2. Upon completion of the whole-class discussion, the teacher distributes a copy of the assessment form (see Figure 4.6) to each small group of

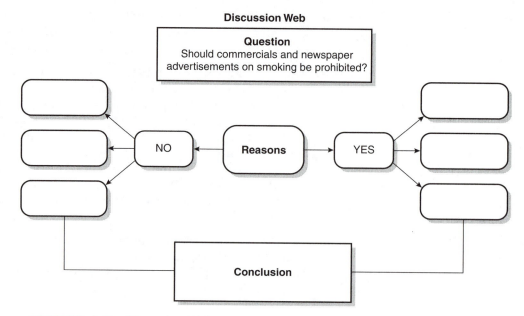

FIGURE 4.5: Discussion Web

students. The teacher should take time to emphasize the importance of self-assessment, especially if the students are not familiar with its purpose. Because the students worked in groups of two, their self-assessments may be conducted together. Each pair receives one rating form.

3. The teacher familiarizes students with the questions and explains how to answer each question using the rating scale and posting their comments, emphasizing the importance of honesty in the process. The teacher has each student think about and rate his or her own performance.

4. After the students have completed the forms, the teacher collects them and assesses the students' performances in the same way. The teacher's assessment may be completed when the students are engaged in the follow-up activities.

5. After the teacher analyzes the students' performances, he or she conducts an individual conference with each student. This conference is short, with focused discussions on helping the student improve in one or two areas.

Professional Resources to Explore

Discussion Strategies Website
www.queensu.ca/idcresources/handouts/discussion_strategies.html
This website offers a number of different strategies to encourage discussion with students.

Fay, K., & Whaley, S. (2004). *Becoming one community: Reading and writing with English language learners.* Portland, ME: Stenhouse.

Gallagher, K. (2003). *Motivational mini-lessons for middle and high school.* Portland, ME: Stenhouse.

References

Alvermann, D. E. (1991). The discussion web: A graphic organizer for learning across the curriculum. *Reading Teacher, 45,* 92–91.

Cazden, C. B. (1988). *Classroom discourse: The language of teaching and learning.* Portsmouth, NH: Heinemann.

Wells, G. (2001). *Action, talk, and text: Learning and teaching through inquiry.* New York: Teachers College Press.

Rating Scale for Discussion Web Activities:
Self-Assessment and Teacher Assessment

Small-Group Members _____   Date _____

Students' Names: S_1 _____ S_2 _____

Directions: Please read each question and answer it by rating yourself using a number between 1 and 10, as it appears on the scale below. You may wish to write a brief comment about your performance.

Far Below Expectations   Exceeds Expectations

1 ————————————————————————— 10

Prereading and Reading	S_1	S_2	T
Did I honestly participate in the prereading discussion?			
Did I set a purpose for reading?			
Was I engaged in reading, critically thinking, and asking questions while I was reading?			
Discussion Web	S_1	S_2	T
Did I participate in the small-group discussion?			
Did I honestly look at both sides of the issue, providing reasons for the "Yes" and the "No" decisions?			
Was I willing to record the reasons on the graphic?			
Group Discussion	S_1	S_2	T
Did I provide a set of arguments to help come to a consensus?			
Was my behavior appropriate for discussion: taking turns, listening, willingness to compromise, voicing my opinions politely?			

COMMENTS: STUDENT$_1$

COMMENTS: STUDENT$_2$

COMMENTS: TEACHER

FIGURE 4.6: Rating Scale for Discussion Web Activities

A Strategy for Developing Comprehension of Text through Discussion

INSTRUCTIONAL CONTEXT				
Grade Level	*Literacy Level*	*Group Size*	*Literature Genre*	*Literacy Skills*
○ K–2	○ Emergent	● Whole class	○ Fiction	● Comprehension
● 2–4	● Early	● 8–10 students	● Nonfiction	● Vocabulary
● 5–6	● Transitional	● 4–6 students		❖ Discussion
● 7–8	● Fluent	● Individual		● Writing
				● Critical thinking

● *Applicable*	○ *Not applicable*	❖ *Target skill*

A Framework for Instruction

The Editor Interview strategy allows teachers to facilitate students' critical thinking through discussion. When schools use talking, reading, and writing for critical thinking and integrating the language arts, students are using language as a tool to work out ideas (Britton, 1970). Research has shown that when the language arts are integrated with content-area material, students develop much denser background knowledge (Beck & Dole, 1992). A rich, elaborate schema is essential for critical thinking as students argue a point or solve an intricate problem.

The Editor Interview strategy requires students to work in pairs or groups as they outline their arguments. Through integration of the language arts and the learning process, language becomes the tool for critical thinking (Vygotsky, 1978; Wells & Chang-Wells, 1994). In this strategy, students work in pairs or groups to develop a logical argument to present in an editorial. When students work together in groups on a critical-thinking activity, they are also learning about language itself (Wells & Chang-Wells, 1994).

The ability to use language as a tool for critical thinking is common among strategic readers (Pressley & Afflebach, 1995). Reading an expository text can be very difficult due to its fact-filled nature, especially for English language learners. However, when students are given extensive exposure to an expository text, they develop the depth and breadth of knowledge necessary to comprehend its meaning (Morrow, Pressley, Smith, & Smith, 1997). This section will describe how to implement Editor Interviews in an intermediate or middle school classroom with students from mixed ability levels.

Learner Outcomes

- The students will argue for or against a position and write an editorial.
- The students will research a topic before they form a position.
- The students will analyze an editor's argument through an interview.

Instructional Procedure

The Editor Interview strategy is a creative way to help students develop an argument and defend it through research. This section describes how to implement this strategy for critical thinking.

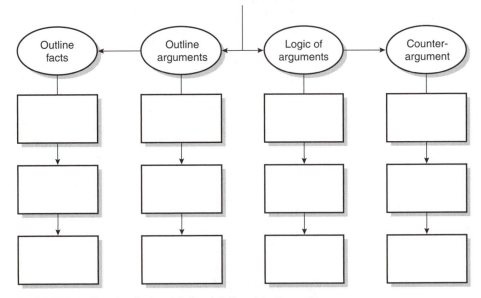

FIGURE 4.7: Analysis of Editorial Graphic Organizer

Step by Step

1. The teacher presents an editorial from a magazine or newspaper for the students to examine. If the students are struggling readers, the teacher might choose an editorial from a news magazine written for children.

2. The teacher uses the graphic organizer illustrated in Figure 4.7 to help the students analyze the argument present in the editorial. English language learners may need additional support for this component.

3. Working as a group, students research a current event and plan an editorial. The students can use the same graphic organizer to brainstorm their editorial. The following questions can be used to begin the session:
   - How would you argue for the position?
   - How would you argue against it?
   - What would convince you to change your mind about the topic?

4. After the groups have finished their editorial, one of the students from each group volunteers to be the "editor" to be interviewed. It is important that the student feels comfortable in the role of editor.

5. The students pose questions to the editor about his or her line of argument. The students posing the questions should have prior knowledge about the topic to inform their queries.

6. After the interview session, the whole class summarizes their current thinking about the topic after having listened to the interview. The response should address whether their thinking has changed about the topic.

An Application of the Editor Interview Strategy for Grade 7

Mr. Spenser's seventh-grade class was debating the civil rights of suspected terrorists arrested and held in the United States. The students were divided into groups and read an editorial from *USA Today* regarding the prisoners held in American prisons on charges of suspected terrorism. Maryanne's group completed the graphic organizer shown in Figure 4.7 and elected Maryanne to be their editor. The students used the focus questions that Mr. Spenser had given them to practice their interview before they presented it to the class.

After all of the students had presented their editorial interviews, Mr. Spenser asked them to write how their thinking had changed about the prisoners as a result of the discussion. The students' responses were written on chart paper and displayed as a reference tool for their written summation assignment. Following are their responses:

HOW OUR THINKING CHANGED

I never thought that some suspects might be innocent.

I did not think of the Bill of Rights as a living document.

Assessment Procedure

The Rubric for Assessing Editor Interviews (Figure 4.8) presents a strategy for teachers to evaluate students' critical thinking and decision making. Teachers may use this rubric developmentally and record students' performances over an academic period.

Step by Step

1. The teacher observes the students' literacy behaviors throughout the activity. The teacher should note if any student is struggling with a particular component of the strategy, such as outlining the argument.

2. The teacher uses the rubric for focused observation and evaluation. The rubric can be used to focus on individual students or on group performances. The teacher can modify the rubric to meet students' instructional needs.

   • Students who consistently demonstrate the benchmark behavior are rated at the *Proficient* level. Students performing at the highest level are on task and present a logical, complete editorial interview.
   • When students' behavior is inconsistent or mastery is not demonstrated, the teacher evaluates them as *Developing*. Students are rated as *Developing* when their performance is not of the highest quality or a few components are somewhat inconsistent.
   • The final level, *Beginning,* is given to students who rarely exhibit the benchmark behavior. The lowest rating is given to students that are unable to complete the editorial interview or to present a logical argument.

3. Teachers may give the rubric to students for self-assessment as they prepare to present their arguments to their peers.

Rubric for Assessing Editor Interviews

Name _____ Date _____

Editorial Elements	Beginning	Developing	Proficient
Research on Topic	Research is incomplete or inaccurate concerning topic.	Research is adequate but does not explore topic in depth.	Research is accurate and in depth, exploring topic and details.
Argument	Argument is illogical and does not use research.	Argument is somewhat logical and based partially on research.	Argument is logical, well thought out, and based on research.
Counter-Argument	Counter-argument is not addressed in editorial.	Counter-argument is partially addressed in editorial.	Counter-argument is addressed in editorial and debated during interview.
Queries during Interview	Queries are not answered.	Some queries are answered by citing research.	Handles queries by citing research and logic.
Interview	Student does not present editorial or address questions from peers.	Student's performance is somewhat accurate.	Student accurately presents argument in editorial and defends position.

SUMMARY OF STUDENT PERFORMANCE

FIGURE 4.8: Rubric for Assessing Editor Interviews

Professional Resources to Explore

New York Times
www.thenewyorktimes.org
This site offers special links for teachers on using the newspaper in the classroom.

British Broadcasting Corporation (BBC)
www.bbc.co.uk
This is a great source of links for teachers to resources from around the world.

Ennis, R. H. (1996). *Critical thinking.* Upper Saddle River, NJ: Prentice Hall.

Luke, A. (2001). Critical literacy in Australia: A matter of context and standpoint. *Journal of Adult and Adolescent Literacy, 43*(5), 448–461.

Tovani, C. (2003). *Thoughtful reading: Teaching comprehension to adolescents.* Portland, ME: Stenhouse.

References

Beck, I., & Dole, J. (1992). Reading and thinking in history and science text. In C. Collins & J. Mangieri (Eds.), *Thinking development: An agenda for the twenty-first century.* Hillsdale, NJ: Erlbaum.

Britton, J. (1970). *Language and learning.* Harmondsworth, England: Penguin.

Morrow, L. M., Pressley, M., Smith, J., & Smith, M. (1997). The effect of a literature based program integrated with literacy and science instruction with children from diverse backgrounds. *Reading Research Quarterly, 32*(1), 54–76.

Pressley, M., & Afflebach, P. (1995). *Verbal protocols in reading: The nature of constructing responsive reading.* Hillsdale, NJ: Erlbaum.

Vygotsky, L. S. (1978). *Mind in society: The development of higher mental processes* (M. Cole, V. John-Steiner, S. Scribner, & E. Souberman, Eds./Trans.). Cambridge, MA: Harvard University Press.

Wells, G., & Chang-Wells, G. L. (1992). *Constructing knowledge together: Classrooms as centers of inquiry and learning.* Portsmouth, NH: Heinemann.

A Strategy for Integrating Critical Thinking and Discussion

INSTRUCTIONAL CONTEXT				
Grade Level	*Literacy Level*	*Group Size*	*Literature Genre*	*Literacy Skills*
○ K–2	○ Emergent	● Whole class	○ Fiction	● Comprehension
● 2–4	● Early	● 8–10 students	● Nonfiction	● Vocabulary
● 5–6	● Transitional	● 4–6 students		❖ Discussion
● 7–8	● Fluent	● Individual		● Writing
				● Critical thinking

● *Applicable*	○ *Not applicable*	❖ *Target skill*

A Framework for Instruction

The Instructional Conversation strategy focuses on factual topics, rather than narrative ones. Having conversations about the topic of study helps students to make personal connections and to generate new ideas (Goldenberg, 1992/1993). When students participate in instructional conversations, they become a community of learners, where every voice is honored (Tompkins, 2004). Students generate questions and explore intricate concepts and ideas. When students explore topics through discussion, they engage in academic discourse.

Academic discourse is a more elaborate language structure, in which children use language to view different perspectives as well as to generate ideas (Antonacci & O'Callaghan, 2004). As students use language to explore ideas, they use it to summarize, clarify, compare, and contrast (Raban, 2001). When language is used for exploration and interpretation, students begin to internalize literate models of thinking and learn how to communicate ideas (Tharp & Gallimore, 1988).

Instructional conversations have been found to help students attain fluency in reading and writing (New Standards Speaking and Listening Committee, 2001). During discussions on academic content, students begin to argue a point as well as to collaborate with others on building understanding (Antonacci & O'Callaghan, 2004). This versatile strategy can be used across the grades and ability levels. This section will describe how to implement instructional conversations in your classroom.

Learner Outcomes

- The students will use dialogue and questioning to construct meaning.
- The students will summarize content and make personal connections.

Instructional Procedure

Instructional conversations are primarily used with expository texts to help students construct meaning. This versatile strategy can be modified to meet the needs of special learners and struggling readers.

Step by Step

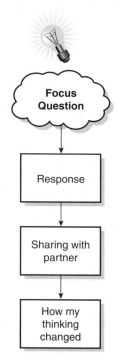

FIGURE 4.9: Sample Graphic Organizer

1. Before students begin this activity, the teacher has to analyze the topic and choose guiding questions. English language learners may need pictures or other materials to activate their prior knowledge.

2. In order to prepare the students for the conversation, the teacher should distribute the graphic organizer illustrated in Figure 4.9, which is to be completed individually. The teacher may choose to pair students who are struggling readers, with students of a higher reading level to aid in the processing of text.

3. After the students have finished their graphic organizers, the classroom is arranged into a circle for the discussion. The teacher may choose to put students in small groups.

4. The teacher begins the conversation by posing a focus question or opening statement. Students may want to write down their responses to the question or statement before the discussion begins.

5. During the discussion, the teacher elaborates on and extends the students' responses. The teacher also writes down the students' major points or opinions on chart paper.

6. The students may refer to their graphic organizers or to prior readings to defend their positions or extend their responses. Students should also be encouraged to write down any responses made by peers that they wish to explore or discuss further.

7. After the discussion, the students write summaries of their new knowledge as a result of the activity. Their responses should include how the discussion helped them to construct meaning or to make a personal connection to the topic.

An Application of the Instructional Conversation Strategy for Grade 4

Mr. William's fourth-grade class has been studying a unit on ecology. They have been researching the food chain for the past two days and are now ready to have their first instructional conversation on the topic. Mr. Williams holds these sessions during practically every unit, and the students always look forward to them.

Today, Mr. Williams has written the focus question on the whiteboard: "Is the food chain in danger?" Several students immediately respond and discuss the new advances in organic farming and genetic engineering of the food supply. Miguel has studied sharks and their place in the food chain, so he contributes to the discussion about the dangers of polluting the oceans. After twenty minutes, the conversation is just beginning to heat up, but Mr. Williams stops it and has the students read the major points they have discussed from the chart paper. After summarizing the instructional conversation, Mr. Williams directs the students back to their seats to write their own summations of the discussion.

Assessment Procedure

The Annotated Checklist for Instructional Conversations (Figure 4.10) can be used to evaluate a student's performance during the discussion. The teacher may want to use the assessment tools in the "Discussion" section of this book (Section Four) as evaluative instruments across subject areas and strategies.

Annotated Checklist for Instructional Conversations

Name _____   Date _____

Critical-Thinking Behaviors	Beginning	Developing	Proficient
Student summarizes content and identifies main idea.			
Student identifies metacognitive strategies to use during reading or discussion.			
Student is aware of peer responses and generates new ideas.			
Student constructs meaning from text and makes personal connections.			

COMMENTS

FIGURE 4.10: Annotated Checklist for Instructional Conversations

Step by Step

1. The teacher observes the students during the activity and focuses on certain students. During the course of one month, every student should be evaluated.

2. The teacher uses the checklist to focus his or her observations. If a student consistently displays the benchmark behavior, the *Proficient* box is checked. If the behavior is not consistently demonstrated, then the *Developing* box is checked. A student's performance is checked as *Beginning* if the behavior is rarely displayed.

3. The checklist should be used periodically to assess students developmentally over the academic year. After analyzing the data, the teacher may want to note if certain sections of the strategy were either too difficult or too easy for the students and to adjust instruction for the next session.

Professional Resources to Explore

Marco Polo
www.marcopolo.org
This is a link from Read–Write–Think, which also offers activities to integrate critical thinking and the language arts.

Harvey, S., & Goudvis, A. (2004). *Strategic thinking.* Portland, ME: Stenhouse.

Sibberson, F., & Szymusiak, K. (2004). *Bringing reading to life: Instruction and conversation, grades 3–6.* Portland, ME: Stenhouse.

Wood, K. D., & Harmon, J. M. (2001). *Strategies for integrating reading and writing in middle and high school classrooms.* Newark, DE: International Reading Association.

References

Antonacci, P., & O'Callaghan, C. (2004). *Portraits of literacy development: Instruction and assessment in a well-balanced literacy program, K–3.* Upper Saddle River, NJ: Merrill.

Goldenberg, C. (1992/1993). Instructional conversations: Promoting comprehension through discussion. *Reading Teacher, 46,* 316–326.

New Standards Speaking and Listening Committee. (2001). *Speaking and listening for preschool through grade 3.* Pittsburgh: National Center on Education and the Economy and the University of Pittsburgh.

Raban, B. (2001). Talking to think, learn and teach. In P. G. Smith (Ed.), *Talking classrooms: Shaping children's learning through oral instruction* (pp. 27–42). Newark, DE: International Reading Association.

Tharp, R., & Gallimore, R. (1988). *Rousing minds to life: Teaching, learning, and schooling in social context.* New York: Cambridge University Press.

Tompkins, G. (2004). *Fifty literacy strategies: Step by step.* Upper Saddle River, NJ: Merrill.

A Strategy for Developing Discussion

INSTRUCTIONAL CONTEXT				
Grade Level	Literacy Level	Group Size	Literature Genre	Literacy Skills
○ K–2	○ Emergent	● Whole class	○ Fiction	● Comprehension
○ 2–4	○ Early	● 8–10 students	● Nonfiction	● Vocabulary
● 5–6	● Transitional	● 4–6 students		❖ Discussion
● 7–8	● Fluent	● Individual		● Writing
				● Critical thinking

● Applicable	○ Not applicable	❖ Target skill

A Framework for Instruction

The Socratic Seminar strategy helps students to actively engage in the processing of text. During Socratic Seminars, students use exploratory talk to process text material. When students engage in discussion, they are problem solving, as they connect new knowledge to prior knowledge (Unrau, 2004). The key to the success of this strategy is that students are participating in generating text comprehension, rather than the traditional transmission approach (Wade & Moje, 2000). According to the National Reading Panel (2000), "Comprehension is an active process that requires an intentional, thoughtful interaction between the reader and the text" (p. 13).

Socratic Seminars also facilitate the development of academic discourse. *Academic discourse* is a more elaborate, complex language structure, in which students use language to present viewpoints, discuss literature, and generate ideas (Antonacci & O'Callaghan, 2004). As students engage in academic discourse, they construct schema and develop the ability to interpret text. The key to the development of strategic reading is to provide students with multiple opportunities to engage in academic discourse, which is vital for their future success in school (Farris, 2001).

This section will describe how to implement Socratic Seminars with students in the intermediate or middle school grades. The procedure may be modified to accommodate students with special needs.

Learner Outcomes

- The students will use dialogue and questioning to construct meaning.
- The students will develop metacognitive strategies to comprehend text.

Instructional Procedure

The Socratic Seminar strategy is primarily used with expository texts to help students construct meaning. However, it can also be modified to incorporate narrative texts.

Step by Step

1. Before the students begin this activity, the teacher has to analyze the text and prepare guiding questions to use during the seminar. If students are struggling or have difficulties with text, the teacher may choose a reading that is on grade level or slightly below.

2. In order to prepare the students for the seminar, the teacher can distribute the graphic organizer illustrated in Figure 4.11, which is to be completed individually. The first two parts are done before reading, and the last two parts are done during reading.

3. After the students have finished their graphic organizers, arrange them into an inner circle and an outer one. The students on the inside will participate in the discussion. The students on the outside will observe the discussion and take notes.

4. Each student in the inner circle is given two tokens. When a student wants to speak, he or she places one of the tokens in the box in the middle. Students are limited to two turns each.

5. The teacher begins the seminar with a guiding question, such as one of the following:
   - What did you think the reading was about?
   - Did you have any problems with the text?
   - How did you solve problems during reading?
   - How will you use the reading?

6. The discussion is limited to twenty minutes. However, the teacher may want to expand it, if the students are near the closure point.

7. After the discussion, the students in the outer circle comment on the seminar. Then all students write summaries of their new knowledge as a result of the activity. Their responses should include how the discussion helped them to construct meaning.

An Application of the Socratic Seminar Strategy for Grade 8

It is Friday morning, and Mr. Kelaher's eighth-grade class has been studying the chapter on the Civil War in their social studies textbook. The class is composed of struggling readers and students with special needs, so the textbook is very difficult for a majority of the pupils. Jorgé is a struggling English language learner who finds that social studies is his most difficult subject. Because his family only recently came to the United States from Mexico, a lot of the topics, such as the Civil War, are very new to him. Mr. Kelaher showed Jorgé how to do a "chapter walk" before reading, so he can use the pictures and graphics to get a sense of the topic before beginning. Jorgé has completed the "think sheet" Mr. Kelaher distributed in preparation for the seminar, as shown in Figure 4.12.

After completing the "think sheet," Jorgé sits in the inner circle and shares his responses with the class. Several students reply that they are also confused by all the dates and names. Miguel suggests that the class should make a *Who's Who in the Civil War* class book with their own illustrations to help them remember all the generals and officials. Mr. Kelaher responds that the idea is fantastic and that the class will tackle the assignment that afternoon.

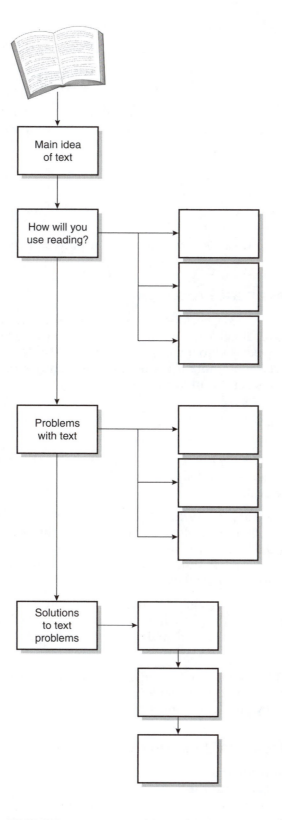

FIGURE 4.11: Sample Graphic Organizer

JORGÉ'S REPLIES FOR THE SOCRATIC SEMINAR

- What did you think the reading was about?
  The chapter was about the causes of the Civil War.

- Did you have any problems with the text?
  There were a lot of dates and names.

- How did you solve problems during reading?
  I drew a timeline like the one we use in class.

- How will you use the reading?
  I will make an outline to study about the war.

FIGURE 4.12: Jorgé's Replies for the Socratic Seminar

Assessment Procedure

The Annotated Checklist for Assessing a Socratic Seminar (Figure 4.13) can be used to evaluate students' performances during a Socratic Seminar. The checklist may be used to focus on an individual student or on a group. However, the teacher should note if a student consistently struggles with the same textual problems across subject areas.

 **Step by Step**

1. The teacher observes the students during the Socratic Seminar and focuses on certain students. During the course of one month, every student should be evaluated.

2. The teacher uses the checklist to focus his or her observations. If a student consistently displays the benchmark behavior, the *Proficient* box is checked. If the behavior is not consistently demonstrated, then the *Developing* box is checked. A student's performance is checked as *Beginning* if the behavior is rarely displayed.

3. The checklist should be used periodically to assess the students developmentally over the academic year. When the checklist is used developmentally, the teacher should analyze the data for patterns across subject areas or text readings.

4. The teacher should note metacognitive strategies. If a student does not use metacognitive strategies, the teacher should demonstrate how to solve literacy problems while reading.

Professional Resources to Explore

Read–Write–Think
www.readwritethink.org
This is a sponsored link of the International Reading Association and offers teachers myriad lesson plans for the development of critical thinking.

Allen, J. (2004). *Tools for teaching content literacy.* Portland, ME: Stenhouse.

Camp, D. (2000). It takes two: Teaching with twin texts of fact and fiction. *Reading Teacher, 53,* 400–408.

Wood, K. D., & Harmon, J. M. (2001). *Strategies for integrating reading and writing in middle and high school classrooms.* Newark, DE: International Reading Association.

Annotated Checklist for Socratic Seminars

Name _____   Date _____

Critical-Thinking Behaviors	Beginning	Developing	Proficient
Student identifies the main idea.			
Student elaborates ideas with specific details.			
Student summarizes the content.			
Student identifies metacognitive strategies to use during reading.			
Student is aware of problems during reading and generates solutions.			
Student constructs meaning from text and analyzes author's content.			

OBSERVATIONAL NOTES AND COMMENTS

FIGURE 4.13: Annotated Checklist for Socratic Seminars

References

Antonacci, P., & O'Callaghan, C. (2004). *Portraits of literacy development: Instruction and assessment in a well-balanced literacy program, K–3.* Upper Saddle River, NJ: Merrill.

Farris, P. (2001). *Language arts process: Process and product and assessment* (3rd ed.). New York: McGraw-Hill.

National Reading Panel. (2000). *Teaching children to read: An evidence-based assessment of the scientific research literature on reading and its implications for reading instruction.* Washington, DC: U.S. Department of Health and Human Services.

Unrau, N. (2004). *Content area reading and writing: Fostering literacies in middle school and high school cultures.* Upper Saddle River, NJ: Merrill.

Wade, S. E., & Moje, E. B. (2000). The role of text in classroom learning. In M. Kamil, P. Mosenthal, P. D. Pearson, & R. Barr (Eds.), *Handbook of reading research* (Vol. 3, pp. 361–380). Mahwah, NJ: Erlbaum.

Instructional and Assessment Strategies for Developing CRITICAL THINKING

Within this section are strategies to help students develop their critical-thinking skills. Although the emphasis is on critical thinking, students will be involved in using other forms of language to complete each activity.

A Strategy for Activating Prior Knowledge for Thinking Critically about Text

INSTRUCTIONAL CONTEXT				
Grade Level	*Literacy Level*	*Group Size*	*Literature Genre*	*Literacy Skills*
O K–1	O Emergent	● Whole class	● Fiction	● Comprehension
O 2–4	O Early	● 8–10 students	● Nonfiction	● Vocabulary
● 5–6	● Transitional	O 4–6 students		● Discussion
● 7–8	● Fluent	O Individual		● Writing
				❖ Critical thinking

● *Applicable*	O *Not applicable*	❖ *Target skill*

A Framework for Instruction

The Anticipation Guide strategy is designed to activate students' prior knowledge in preparing them to read (Readence, Bean, & Baldwin, 1998). Students are asked to think about debatable statements and to agree or disagree, based on their knowledge of the topic and personal experiences. With this starting point, students react to the topic and predict the content that they will be reading and discussing. Therefore, *anticipation guides* have been referred to as *prediction guides* (Richardson & Morgan, 1997). The discussion of the statements is intended to motivate the students to read to resolve any conceptual differences they may have. After the students read the text, there is a follow-up discussion based on the initial statements. Tierney and Readence (2000) suggest that the Anticipation Guide strategy may be used within the postreading discussion to encourage students to deal with new and old information by helping them to resolve any conceptual conflicts, misconceptions, or erroneous information that were raised during their initial discussions.

Strategic readers use their prior knowledge while reading to help them construct new meanings from the text. Often, students do not understand what they are reading because they simply do not know that they need to consider the text in light of what they already know. Through a prereading discussion of the statements in the anticipation guide, students activate their prior knowledge related to the concepts within the reading. Another benefit of the anticipation guide used in the prereading discussion is that it provides a purpose for reading (Gunning, 2003).

Although the purpose of the Anticipation Guide strategy is to activate prior knowledge and help establish a purpose for reading, not all materials will stimulate an active or lively discussion because not all topics are debatable. Further, students may have very little knowledge of the material that they will be reading, and they will become frustrated if asked to generate a position on a statement about which they know little or nothing. Thus, the use of anticipation guides may not be effective for all reading materials.

Learning Outcomes

- Students will participate in a prereading discussion using their prior knowledge to discuss anticipation guide statements related to their readings.

- Students will read for understanding and think critically about the prereading discussion statements.
- Students will participate in a postreading discussion, confirming or rejecting their prereading statements by using new information derived from their reading.

Instructional Procedure

The Anticipation Guide strategy provides a structured approach to facilitate teachers in guiding their students (a) to activate their prior knowledge, (b) to set purposes for reading, and (c) to clear up misconceptions of concepts or content that they may have prior to their reading and discussions.

Step by Step

1. The teacher begins by developing the anticipation guide. The guide consists of open-ended statements related to the reading that will foster discussion by the students. The steps in developing the statements for the anticipation guide are as follow:
   a. Identify the major concepts that will be taught in the lesson and included in the readings.
   b. Identify the students' background knowledge and cultural experiences related to the readings.
   c. Write open-ended statements that foster discussion. The statements are critical in promoting an active discussion. Therefore, the statements need to be thought provoking, encouraging students to respond by activating their background knowledge. Ryder and Graves (2003) emphasize that in constructing the statements, the teacher should *avoid* those that are narrow and that "focus on details or factual information that are removed from students' life experiences or their prior knowledge. Statements should be general enough to elicit diverse points of view based on the various backgrounds of your students" (pp. 134–135). Therefore, statements should not lead to yes and no answers or prompt the recall of facts. Statements for the anticipation guide should promote critical thinking.

2. Arrange the statements from simple to more difficult. The statements may be displayed on the chalkboard, on a large sheet of chart paper, on overhead transparencies, or in a handout.

3. Conduct an interactive prereading discussion based on the anticipation guide statements. Present each statement and encourage students to examine how their own experiences are related to the statement. Tell students that their agreement or disagreement with a statement should be supported by their background knowledge or personal experiences. Successful teacher responses to students within the prereading discussion encourage critical thinking and do not reject student responses as either *right* or *wrong*.

4. The teacher directs the students to read text that is about the statements they discussed. The readings should promote students' thinking about their points of view.

5. After students have completed the reading, the teacher directs them to return to the statements. The teacher conducts the postreading discussion, encouraging the students to revisit their prereading positions on the statements using new information obtained from their reading. Many students will change their positions in light of the new information.

6. To extend student learning, the teacher may include a follow-up activity. Students may be asked to use the new information from their reading and the postreading discussion to rewrite or expand on their position statements.

An Application of the Anticipation Guide for Grade 8

In Millie Otto's eighth-grade social studies class, the students have been studying the roles of city and state governments in creating laws to protect citizens. They are about to read an article from the local newspaper that describes the steps taken in their own city to ban all cigarette smoking in public places, including restaurants, bars, and social clubs. Prior to their reading, the teacher has developed the anticipation guide found in Figure 5.1. She uses these questions, one at a time, to guide the prereading discussion.

After the discussion, the students read the article and revisit the questions. In the postreading discussion, new information from reading the newspaper article has led some students to change their positions on the statements, while other students have elaborated their position statements with new information.

Assessment Procedure

During the Anticipation Guide strategy, the teacher will assess students' discussion skills, their activation and use of prior knowledge in responding to the statements, and their integration of new information from reading and discussion with their prior knowledge. When this strategy is used with the whole class, the teacher may decide to target a small group to observe for assessing and documenting discussion skills.

Step by Step

1. The teacher prepares the assessment forms. For each student who will be assessed, one form is prepared, as shown in Figure 5.2.

ANTICIPATION GUIDE

"Banning the Use of Tobacco in Public Places"

1. The government should take a more aggressive role in banning all smoking because it would benefit society's health and welfare, including its economy.

      Agree_____   Disagree_____

2. When young people know what is good for them and bad for them, they will respond appropriately.

      Agree_____   Disagree_____

3. Smoking should be banned from all public places (restaurants, bars, parks, malls, and wherever people gather) because of the harmful effects of second-hand smoke.

      Agree_____   Disagree_____

FIGURE 5.1: Anticipation Guide for "Banning the Use of Tobacco in Public Places"

Observation of Students Using the Anticipation Guide for Discussion

Student's Name _____   Date _____

Text _____

Element	Observed	Not Observed
Actively participates in discussion.		
Uses discussion skills appropriately.		
Demonstrates use of prior knowledge in responding to statements.		
Reads assigned text for meaning and understanding.		
Upon completion of assigned reading, revisits prereading responses using information from readings.		
Demonstrates increased knowledge through an informed justification for responses.		

SUMMARY OF STUDENT PERFORMANCE

OBSERVATION NOTES AND COMMENTS

FIGURE 5.2: Observation of Students Using the Anticipation Guide for Discussion

2. During discussion, the teacher observes a small group of students. During the discussion, the teacher observes, assesses, and documents students' discussion skills, their responses to statements, and their readings of the assigned text. Using the assessment form in Figure 5.2, the teacher marks each student's competencies.

3. After the students' have completed their written positions to the statements on the anticipation guide, the teacher collects and evaluates them. The teacher assesses the student's responses to the statements and makes comments about the quality of thinking the student demonstrates in using the reading to refute or support his or her position statement.

Professional Resources to Explore

McMackin, M. C., & Siegel, B. S. (2002). *Knowing how: Researching and writing nonfiction, 3–8.* Portland, ME: Stenhouse.

Tovani, C. (2004). *Do I really have to teach comprehension? Content comprehension, grades 6–12.* Portland, ME: Stenhouse.

References

Gunning, T. G. (2003). *Creating literacy instruction for all children* (4th ed.). Boston: Allyn & Bacon.

Readence, J. E., Bean, T. W., & Baldwin, R. S. (1998). *Content area reading: An integrated approach* (6th ed.). Dubuque, IA: Kendall/Hunt.

Richardson, J. S., & Morgan, R. R. (1997). *Reading to learn in the content areas* (3rd ed.). New York: Wadsworth.

Ryder, R. J., & Graves, M. F. (2003). *Reading and learning in content areas* (3rd ed.). New York: John Wiley.

Tierney, R. J., & Readence, J. E. (2000). *Reading strategies and practices: A compendium.* Boston: Allyn & Bacon.

A Strategy for Organizing Information for Understanding and Use

INSTRUCTIONAL CONTEXT				
Grade Level	*Literacy Level*	*Group Size*	*Literature Genre*	*Literacy Skills*
○ K–1	○ Emergent	● Whole class	● Fiction	● Comprehension
● 2–4	● Early	● 8–10 students	● Nonfiction	● Vocabulary
● 5–6	● Transitional	● 4–6 students		● Discussion
● 7–8	● Fluent	● Individual		● Writing
				❖ Critical thinking

● *Applicable*	○ *Not applicable*	❖ *Target skill*

A Framework for Instruction

The Data Chart strategy uses a graphic organizer to help students sort information from different text sources into categories. The arrangement of information into categories facilitates students' comprehension and recall of concepts and ideas and assists them in organizing data for expository writing. The use of questions by the teacher with data charts to assist students in gathering information also promotes their critical-thinking and problem-solving skills, as they are encouraged to locate and integrate new information in responding.

When students attempt to collect the information and retrieve the facts needed for writing a research paper or an essay, they frequently do not know where to begin. Common problems that they face in report writing are identifying the information they need and organizing it for use in their writing. To help students avoid these pitfalls, McKenzie (1979) proposes the use of data charts or comparison charts, which assist young readers and writers by providing a visual display of information in a structured system.

This strategy has been used with different text types. Typically, the charts are used when reading expository or nonfiction texts; however, they have been used when organizing information for literature focus units, such as studying the works of a single author or comparing multiple versions of a folk tale (Tompkins, 2003). For younger students, the Data Chart strategy is used in a more structured way with explicit directions from the teacher. As students become more proficient in the use of these charts, they will employ them with greater flexibility and across a variety of applications. The key to implementation of the Data Chart strategy with all students—younger and older and at varying literacy levels—is the procedure the teacher follows. When teachers consistently help students to think about the information by categorizing it appropriately, students are more apt to achieve higher levels of comprehension. Further, when the Data Chart strategy is used as part of a discussion group with teacher-posed and student-generated questions, students' acquisition of knowledge develops systematically while they learn useful study habits.

Learner Outcomes

- The students will use a systematic approach to research a topic.
- The students will use data charts appropriately to collect information about a topic.

Instructional Procedure

It is important that students understand how to use data charts when reading for information. Guiding students in designing data charts will achieve this goal and help them understand the process of using data charts to gather information.

Step by Step

1. The teacher constructs the data chart to fit the lesson. Design the chart so that it takes on the purpose of the lesson. Then work with students to develop their own data charts or a group data chart. If students are working collaboratively on the same topic, all of their data charts will have the same questions or categories. If they are working on their own topics or aspects of a topic, their charts will differ. This element of the strategy is very important and requires discussion and questioning so that students understand what types of information they are researching. If the students are not familiar with data charts and research, work together as a class on the same data chart, guiding them through the process.

2. The teacher works with students to create a class data chart. On a large sheet of chart paper, work with students to duplicate the data chart. This is especially helpful for younger students in the primary grades or in the early stages of reading and writing. They will need a more structured approach and guidance in the use of data charts. A large-group data chart may be used by the teacher to model the approach and to use together with the class. Alternative ways for creating group data charts include working on transparencies and projecting the chart via computer on a large screen.

3. The teacher may use data charts in many different literacy contexts to help students organize their information. It is easy to understand how data charts may be used to gather information on topics from social studies and science using informational books. Data charts also may be used with fiction, however. For example, when students are learning about characterization and compare traits of characters from the same or different pieces of literature, the chart may be useful.

4. Across the top of the data chart, the teacher lists the categories of information that students are exploring. These categories may be in the form of a phrase or a question.

5. Down the left side of the chart, the teacher lists qualities of the person, place, or object that is being described. For some data charts, the sources of information may be more appropriate to list. For example, when different information is being collected from different sources about a single person or event, it would be more appropriate to list the source, as shown in Figure 5.3.

DATA CHART

Topic: Human Digestive System

Source	Its role in helping humans live	Parts of the digestive system and their functions	Ways to promote a healthy digestive system	Diseases related to the digestive system
Text book: Chapter 2				
Encyclopedias				
Websites				
Trade books				
Magazines				

FIGURE 5.3: Data Chart for Human Digestive System

An Application of the Data Chart Strategy for Grade 5

The students in the fifth-grade at Flag School were engaged in a science unit on the human digestive system. To help students research, collect, and organize information, Mr. Gentile guided them in the development of a data chart. They first decided the different subtopics of the human digestive system that they would research. These subtopics were written in the first row at the top of the data chart. The various sources of information came next. The students decided what sources of information were available to them that would contain information on the human digestive system. In the first column from the left, they wrote the source from which they would gather information. Figure 5.3 shows the beginning of the data chart developed for research on the human digestive system by this fifth-grade class.

Assessment Procedure

The purpose for using data charts with students is to help them to learn to collect information from a variety of text and multimedia sources; to read widely to learn about a topic and then organize the information into categories; and to use the information to write about the topic. The teacher is interested in helping the students learn about researching a topic in more systematic ways. Therefore, the teacher will need to monitor how the students are using data charts to collect information from a variety of sources.

Step by Step

1. Use the assessment form in Figure 5.4 for each student or for a group of students, if they are working collaboratively. Note that the assessment form identifies various sources of information that students will use to collect information. The form may be adjusted for use with different topics that demand using varied sources for research.

2. Prepare the forms in advance, at the beginning of the unit of study. For each student, have a form that is filled out in advance.

3. During the course of the unit of study, observe students as they engage in research using the data charts for collecting information. On each student's form, mark the level of proficiency in conducting research from each source. Anecdotal information may be noted on the form, as well, including areas for improvement, strategies that the student has developed, and so on.

4. As often as possible, assess students for their methods of research and date all such observations. The assessment form may be used to help students by providing mini-lessons on research to a small group of students or to the whole class. The form also may be used to help create a literacy profile for each child.

Professional Resources to Explore

Data Charts and Critical-Thinking Websites
www.winslow-jhs.u52.k12.me.us/perry/data.htm
This website offers different templates of data charts to use with the following data sources: books, reference books, encyclopedias, magazine and newspaper articles, online encyclopedias, and the World Wide Web.

www.scholar.lib.vt.edu/ejournals/JTE/jte-7n1/gokhale.jte-7n1.html
This site contains an article on the development of critical thinking through collaborative learning.

Armstrong, P. (2000). *Information transformation: Teaching strategies for authentic research, projects, and activities.* Portland, ME: Stenhouse.

Jobe, R., & Dayton-Sakari, M. (2001). *Info-kids: How to use nonfiction to turn reluctant readers into enthusiastic learners.* Portland, ME: Stenhouse.

Rubric for Assessing the Use of Data Charts

Student's Name _____   Grade _____

Topic _____   Date _____

SOURCE OF INFORMATION	LOCATES INFORMATION	READS FOR MEANING	RECORDS INFORMATION ACCURATELY
Textbook			
Literature			
Encyclopedia			
Online Encyclopedia			
Magazine			
Newspaper			
Website			

Comments:

KEY

B: Beginning Skills—Student is beginning to use the data charts and often relies on the assistance of the teacher. Makes many errors in using data charts as a research tool.

D: Developing Skills—Student is developing skills in using the data charts and seldom relies on the assistance of the teacher. Makes few errors in using data charts as a research tool.

P: Proficient Skills—Student is proficient using data charts and does not need the assistance of the teacher. Makes no errors in using data charts as a research tool.

A: Advanced—Student demonstrates an advanced level of performance by modifying the data chart to include additional sources and topics of related information. Makes no errors in use of data charts and works with other students in helping them to use data charts.

FIGURE 5.4: Rubric for Assessing the Use of Data Charts

References

McKenzie, G. R. (1979). Data charts: A crutch for helping pupils organize reports. *Language Arts, 56,* 784–788.

Tompkins, G. E. (2003). *Fifty literacy strategies: Step by step.* Upper Saddle River, NJ: Merrill/Prentice Hall.

A Strategy for Developing Inferences

INSTRUCTIONAL CONTEXT				
Grade Level	*Literacy Level*	*Group Size*	*Literature Genre*	*Literacy Skills*
○ K–2	○ Emergent	● Whole class	● Fiction	● Comprehension
● 2–4	● Early	● 8–10 students	○ Nonfiction	● Vocabulary
● 5–6	● Transitional	● 4–6 students		● Discussion
● 7–8	● Fluent	● Individual		● Writing
				❖ Critical thinking

● Applicable	○ Not applicable	❖ Target skill

A Framework for Instruction

The Literature Report Card strategy helps students to construct inferences about character traits in a story and to defend their choices based on text references (Whisler & Williams, 1990). After students read a story, they analyze the main character's traits, attribute a grade to each trait, and substantiate their decision with evidence from the text.

In 2000, the National Reading Panel identified the seven most effective comprehension strategies used by readers. The ability to make an inference was included in the "effective" category, and the panel recommended that teachers provide instruction in making inferences. There are two types of inferences that readers can construct while comprehending text. The first type involves deducing relationships in text, such as character traits and how they lead to actions. The second type occurs when readers infer implicit information based on their prior knowledge (Armbuster & Osborn, 2002). The following section outlines the procedure for this instructional activity.

Learner Outcomes

- The students will read fiction and infer character traits.
- The students will work collaboratively to evaluate the characters on determined traits and defend their choices to the class.

Instructional Procedure

The Literature Report Card strategy facilitates students' ability to make inferences and can be used across ability levels. If the majority of students are struggling readers, the teacher might want to use a story on a lower reading level to introduce this strategy.

Step by Step

1. After finishing the story, the class brainstorms the main character's traits using the character web illustrated in Figure 5.5. English language learners may need additional support to complete the first component.

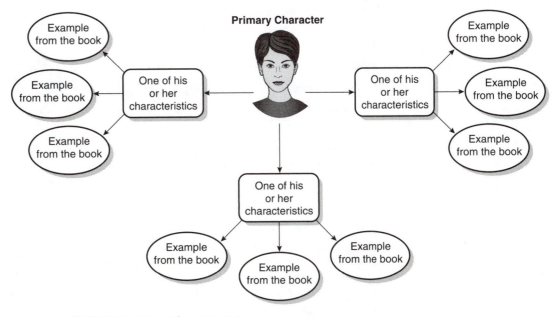

FIGURE 5.5: Character Map

2. After the class has finished completing the character web, they break into groups of four and begin to select the character traits they will use in their Literature Report Cards. If students need to refer to the text, they should be encouraged to do so.

3. Once character traits have been selected, each group assigns a grade to each trait and writes their rationale for the assessment. They also include an excerpt from the text to support their assessment (see Figure 5.6).

4. After the groups have completed their Literature Report Cards, they present their work to the class and defend their choices.

An Application of the Literature Report Card Strategy for Grade 6

Mrs. Willner's sixth-grade class has been engrossed in a literature unit on *Great Expectations*, by Charles Dickens. According to assessment data from their previous author study, the students need to work on making inferences. Mrs. Willner has decided to implement the Literature Report Card strategy to help struggling students learn from their peers about using prior knowledge to construct inferences.

The students are placed in mixed-ability groups and given the character web to discuss. Each group is allowed to select the character they want to focus on for the web. Carla's group votes to select Pip as the focus of their Literature Report Card. After using their books to complete the character webs, the students discuss the traits they will evaluate on the Literature Report Card. Carla's group completes the report card shown in Figure 5.7. Several other groups have also selected Pip, so there is a lively debate on which traits are dominant. Mrs. Willner is very pleased to see students defending their choices by reading aloud from the book. After analyzing the assessment data, Mrs. Willner is encouraged that several students have improved in making inferences. However, there is still a core group struggling with this skill, so the Literature Report Card Strategy will be used with another book.

LITERATURE REPORT CARD

Harry Potter

Group Names   Linda, Kerry, Daniel, Maria

Character Traits	Grade	Character Actions	Evidence from Text
brave	A	Harry fought Lord Voldermort.	Page 358
intelligent	B	Harry figures out ways to escape.	Page 291
emotional	B	Harry gets angry at Draco Malfoy.	Page 49
magical	A	Harry can make magic.	Page 141

FIGURE 5.6: Literature Report Card for *Harry Potter*

LITERATURE REPORT CARD

Pip

Group: Carla, Sherri, Paul, Kendra, and Jamal

Character Traits	Grade	Character Actions	Evidence from Text
foolish	A	Pip did a lot of silly things.	Page 48
weak	B	Pip let the others walk over him.	Page 73
emotional	B	Pip falls in love easily.	Page 36

FIGURE 5.7: Literature Report Card for *Great Expectations*

Self-Assessment of the Literature Report Card

Name _____　　Date _____

Title of Book _____　　Author _____

Performance Indicators	Always	Sometimes	Never
Generates character traits.			
Analyzes and evaluates character traits.			
Offers evidence from text to support claims about character.			
Works well with others in groups.			

SCALE FOR ASSESSING YOUR WORK:

Always: "I can do it on my own all the time. I can explain it to others who need help."
Sometimes: "I can do it by myself sometimes, but I might ask for help from the teacher or my friends."
Never: "This is too hard for me to do by myself, so my friends or the teacher helps me."

THIS IS WHAT I LEARNED FROM MY CLASSMATES:

FIGURE 5.8: Self-Assessment of the Literature Report Card

Assessment Procedure

The purpose of the Self-Assessment of the Literature Report Card (Figure 5.8) is for students to evaluate their own performances on this activity.

Step by Step

1. The teacher observes the students' literacy behaviors throughout the activity to offer feedback to each student. The self-assessment instrument may be used by the teacher over the course of a semester to note each student's developmental progress.

2. The teacher demonstrates to the students how to use the self-assessment form by explaining this rating scale:
   - *Always:* "I perform this task with no help from my friends or the teacher. I can explain it to others who need help."
   - *Sometimes:* "I understand the task, but sometimes I need the help from someone in my group or the teacher."
   - *Never:* "This is a task that I find difficult. I need the help of my friends or the teacher, and I can't do it by myself."

3. The teacher may choose to distribute assessment forms to the whole class for feedback from their peers, as well. Feedback from peers is very useful for improving student performance. Students learn to listen to their peers' comments to improve their work before it is ready for presentation.

Professional Resources to Explore

Speaking and Listening Skills to Preschool through Grade 3 Students
www.ncee.org
This site offers instructional strategies for oral language.

Berko, G. (2001). *The development of language* (5th ed.). Boston: Allyn & Bacon.

Daniels, H. (2002). *Literature circles: Voice and choice in book clubs and reading groups.* Portland, ME: Stenhouse.

McCabe, A. (1996). *Chameleon readers: Teaching children to appreciate all kinds of good stories.* New York: McGraw-Hill.

References

Armbuster, B., & Osborn, J. H. (2002). *Reading instruction and assessment.* Boston: Allyn & Bacon.

National Reading Panel. (2000). *Teaching children to read: An evidence-based assessment of the scientific research literature on reading and its implications for reading instruction.* Washington, DC: National Institute of Child Health and Human Development.

Whisler, N., & Williams, J. (1990). *Literature and cooperative learning: Pathways to literacy.* Sacramento, CA: Literature Co-Op.

Children's Literature References

Dickens, C. (1861/1995). *Great expectations.* New York: Puffin Books.

Rowling, J. K. (1998). *Harry Potter and the sorcerer's stone.* New York: Scholastic.

A Strategy for Developing Critical Thinking

INSTRUCTIONAL CONTEXT				
Grade Level	**Literacy Level**	**Group Size**	**Literature Genre**	**Literacy Skills**
O K–2	O Emergent	● Whole class	O Fiction	● Comprehension
O 2–4	O Early	● 8–10 students	● Nonfiction	● Vocabulary
● 5–6	● Transitional	● 4–6 students		● Discussion
● 7–8	● Fluent	● Individual		● Writing
				❖ Critical thinking

● *Applicable*	O *Not applicable*	❖ *Target skill*

A Framework for Instruction

The Presenting an Argument strategy enables students to discuss both sides of an argument and then to write a coherent, logical essay on the topic. Students in the intermediate and middle school grades are often required to write essays on current events and controversial topics. Unfortunately, many students are not prepared to present an argument logically in writing.

When students research and discuss controversial issues and current events, they are engaging in *academic discourse,* a more complex language structure that requires students to argue a point, generate ideas, or discuss literature (Antonacci & O'Callaghan, 2004). When students engage in varied experiences of interpreting and defending points of view, they begin to master academic discourse. The ability to argue a point logically and coherently is an essential skill for high school coursework and beyond. Engaging in academic discourse also facilitates the construction of schemata as well as the ability to interpret text (Tharp & Gallimore, 1988).

This instructional activity requires students to work in pairs and to explore both sides of an issue. After researching, discussing, and exploring a topic, the students are required to write essays presenting their arguments. Research has shown that when reading and writing are integrated through instruction, critical thinking is more present than when either process is presented alone (Braunger & Lewis, 1997).

Reading and writing are easily integrated with critical thinking, due to the fact that they share similar cognitive processes, such as brainstorming, problem solving, and composing (Tierney & Shanahan, 1991). Both processes are complex as well as goal directed and incorporate multiple subprocesses (Flower & Hayes, 1981). When students read and write for a variety of purposes, they gain mastery of both processes (Atwell, 1987; Calkins, 1991).

The Presenting an Argument strategy allows students to discuss, problem solve, and generate ideas as they develop a logical rationale to support a thesis statement (Unrau, 2004). As they argue and compose, their critical thinking is expanded as well as their knowledge base.

Learner Outcomes

- The students will generate the pros/cons of a topic or controversial issue.
- The students will discuss their thesis statements and edit their arguments.
- The students will create persuasive essays to support their thesis statements.

Instructional Procedure

The Presenting an Argument strategy facilities students' ability to think critically. English language learners and struggling readers may need additional preparation regarding the content for this strategy. Another modification of the lesson would be to pair students who have special needs with peers on a higher reading level. This section will describe how to implement the strategy.

Step by Step

1. Place students in pairs, and ask them to research a controversial topic or issue. The teacher may choose to pair the children heterogeneously so they can support one another. Students may choose the topic, or the teacher can select one from current events.

2. After researching the topic, each student decides to defend either the pro or the con side of the topic. If the student cannot choose a side, the teacher may assign one.

3. Students use the "think sheet" illustrated in Figure 5.9 to organize their thoughts on the topic. English language learners and struggling readers may need additional support.

4. Students identify supporting details for their side of the argument and add them to the chart. Students should be encouraged to use reference materials to research supporting details.

5. Working together, the students critique one another's arguments and eliminate any ideas that are not supported or are unclear. The teacher may need to model how to critique an argument when introducing this strategy.

6. When students finish their critiques, they are ready to complete the graphic organizer displayed in Figure 5.10 to plan their persuasive essays.

7. Partners edit their essay and prepare to present it to the class. The students may use the rubric in this strategy to prepare their essays.

8. After the student partners present their essays to the class, their peers critique their arguments with the rubric in Figure 5.12. The students may use the critique to note how they can improve their thesis statements.

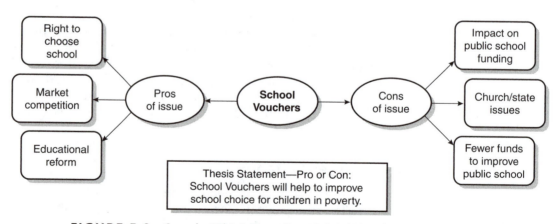

FIGURE 5.9: Sample "Think Sheet" on School Vouchers

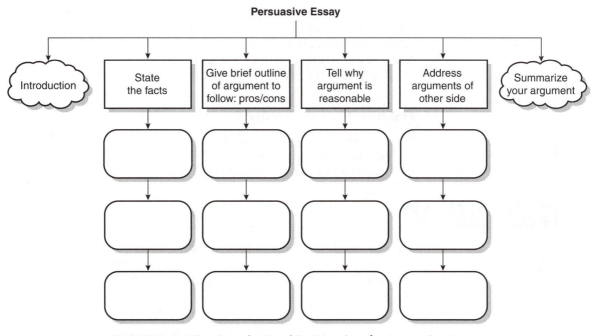

FIGURE 5.10: Sample Graphic Organizer for Persuasive Essay

An Application of the Presenting an Argument Strategy for Grade 8

Jennifer and Tonya have been working on their persuasive essay for several days now. Their eighth-grade teacher, Mr. Carlos, assigned them the topic of school vouchers to present to the class. Jennifer and Tonya have spent time researching the arguments pro/con regarding school vouchers and used the graphic organizer shown in Figure 5.11 to write their essay. After they completed the

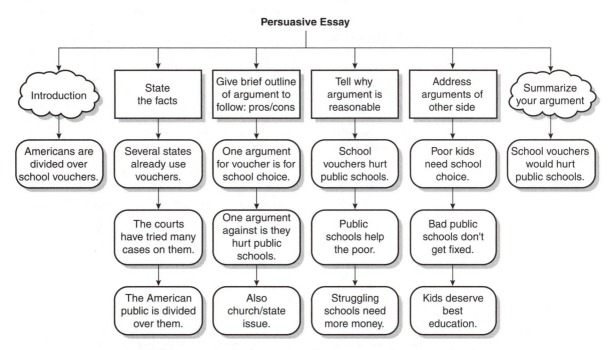

FIGURE 5.11: Students' Graphic Organizer for Persuasive Essay

graphic organizer, Mr. Carlos asked them to exchange it with that of another group for a critique. Their peers commented that they needed to elaborate on the argument against school vouchers. After revising their work, Jennifer and Tonya were ready to write their persuasive essay on school vouchers and felt confident that their argument was logical.

Assessment Procedure

The purpose of the rubric (Figure 5.12) is to sharpen students' awareness of a logical, coherent argument. As each pair presents their essay, the other students may use the following rubric to critique their work.

Step by Step

1. The teacher observes the students' behaviors throughout the activity. If students are working in pairs or groups, the teacher may want to focus on certain individual students on a rotating basis.

Rubric for Assessing Presenting an Argument

Name _____   Date _____

Benchmark Behaviors	Beginning	Developing	Proficient
Research on Topic	Little or no research is included in the essay.	Research is somewhat present and some facts are included.	Topic is thoroughly researched and facts are clearly presented.
Thesis Statement	Argument lacks a thesis statement.	A partial thesis statement is included.	Thesis statement is logical and coherent.
Supporting Details	No supporting details are provided.	The thesis statement is partially described or mentioned.	The thesis statement is fully supported through details.
Sides of Topic	The argument does not address the opposing viewpoint.	There is a partial description of both sides of the issue.	Both sides of the argument are presented and described.
Presentation of Ideas	Argument is illogical or incoherent.	Ideas are presented in a somewhat logical and coherent manner.	Ideas are presented in a logical and coherent manner.

OVERALL CRITIQUE OF ARGUMENT

FIGURE 5.12: Rubric for Assessing Presenting an Argument

2. The teacher uses the rubric shown in Figure 5.12 for focused observation and evaluation. Instead of evaluating the student at the end of the lesson, the teacher should focus on the benchmark performance in each component:

   - Students who consistently demonstrate the benchmark behavior are rated on the *Proficient* level. Students at this level perform the benchmark behavior with ease or perform beyond grade-level expectations.
   - When students' behavior is inconsistent or mastery is not demonstrated, the teacher evaluates them as *Developing*. Students are evaluated as *Developing* when they are unable to perform one or two of the components.
   - The final level, *Beginning*, is given to students who rarely exhibit the benchmark behavior. The rating of *Beginning* is given to students who are unable to perform the benchmark behaviors or can only do one task.

3. The teacher may give the rubric to students for self-assessment as they prepare to present their arguments to their peers.

Professional Resources to Explore

Read–Write–Think
www.readwritethink.org
This is a sponsored link of the International Reading Association and offers teachers myriad lesson plans for the development of critical thinking.

Langer, E. (1997). *The power of mindful learning.* Reading, MA: Addison-Wesley.

Novak, J. D. (1998). *Learning, creating, and using knowledge: Concept maps as facilitative tools in schools and corporations.* Mahwah, NJ: Erlbaum.

Sibberson, F., & Szymusiak, K. (2004). *Bringing reading to life: Instruction and conversation, grades 3–6.* Portland, ME: Stenhouse.

References

Antonacci, P., & O'Callaghan, C. (2004). *Portraits of literacy development: Instruction and assessment in a well-balanced literacy program, K–3.* Upper Saddle River, NJ: Pearson/Merrill.

Atwell, N. (1987). *In the middle: Writing, reading, and learning with adolescents.* Portsmouth, NH: Heinemann.

Braunger, J., & Lewis, J. P. (1997). *Building a knowledge base in reading.* Portland, OR: Northwest Regional Educational Laboratory.

Calkins, L. M. (1991). *Living between the lines.* Portsmouth, NH: Heinemann.

Flower, L, & Hayes, J. R. (1981). A cognitive process theory of writing. *College Composition and Communication, 32,* 365–387.

Tharp, R., & Gallimore, R. (1988). *Rousing minds to life: Teaching, learning and schooling in social context.* New York: Cambridge University Press.

Tierney, R. J., & Shanahan, T. (1991). Research on the reading-writing relationship: Interactions, transactions and outcomes. In R. Barr, M. L. Kamil, P. Mosenthal, & P. D. Pearson (Eds.), *Handbook of reading research* (Vol. 2, pp. 246–280). New York: Longman.

Unrau, N. (2004). *Content area reading and writing: Fostering literacies in middle and high school cultures.* Upper Saddle River, NJ: Pearson.

A Strategy for Developing Critical Thinking

INSTRUCTIONAL CONTEXT				
Grade Level	*Literacy Level*	*Group Size*	*Literature Genre*	*Literacy Skills*
○ K–2	○ Emergent	● Whole class	● Fiction	● Comprehension
○ 2–4	○ Early	● 8–10 students	● Nonfiction	● Vocabulary
● 5–6	● Transitional	○ 4–6 students		● Discussion
● 7–8	● Fluent	○ Individual		● Writing
				❖ Critical thinking

● *Applicable*	○ *Not applicable*	❖ *Target skill*

A Framework for Instruction

The Think–Pair–Share strategy integrates questioning and responding to text to promote critical thinking. In this activity, the teacher poses a critical-thinking question, and the student writes a response and shares it with a partner (Unrau, 2004). When teachers pose questions, they keep students on task, focus them on what is to be learned, elicit active processing of text, and activate metacognitive processing of content (Armbruster & Osborn, 2002).

Instructional conversations such as Think–Pair–Share, which integrate questioning and responding, are effective in improving critical thinking. According to constructivist theory, learning is primarily a social activity (Vygotsky, 1962). Instructional conversations allow students to engage in sociocultural contexts that are inherently communicative as they process text (Wertsch, 1991). As students talk and respond to text, they transform their understanding of content and also internalize the process (Rogoff, 1995). This internalization of questioning and responding to text is the key to development of metacognition in students.

Posing critical-thinking questions during all three phases of reading (before, during, and after) is especially effective for struggling readers (Hansen & Pearson, 1983). When teachers engage students in questioning, they are using one of the most influential teaching acts (Armbruster & Osborn, 2002). In addition, Think–Pair–Share allows students to go back and reread content to write a response, which is another way to improve critical thinking (Garner, Hare, Alexander, Hynes, & Winograd, 1984). The National Reading Panel (2000) presented a strong research base that supports students' generating their own questions during reading. Engaging students to gradually take on the role of facilitator during this activity is one way to promote student generation of questions.

Think–Pair–Share has been used by teachers at all grade levels and found to be an effective strategy for engaging students in instructional conversations. As students respond to critical-thinking questions, they begin to internalize the question–response process. This internalization leads to metacognition and the generation of questions. Recent research has found particular value in instructional conversations as central mechanisms for the development of language in students who are at risk for literacy failure (Goldenberg, 1996). The following section will describe how to implement Think–Pair–Share in the literacy classroom.

Learner Outcomes

- The students will use dialogue and questioning to construct meaning.
- The students will develop metacognitive strategies to comprehend text.
- The students will generate their own questions about the text.

Instructional Procedure

Think–Pair–Share is an excellent strategy to help students actively process text material. This section will describe how to implement the strategy.

Step by Step

1. Before the students begin this activity, the teacher has to analyze the text and prepare a key critical-thinking question. The teacher might want to use easier text for struggling readers to help them learn this strategy.

2. In order to facilitate the processing of text, the teacher should distribute the graphic organizer displayed in Figure 5.13 to the students.

3. After students have completed the "Response" section of their graphic organizers, they are put into pairs to begin their instructional conversations. The teacher may want to pair students of mixed abilities.

4. Students share their responses with their partners and then write one response as a team. English language learners may need more support for this component.

5. The teacher leads the class in sharing their responses with their peers. The teacher or a student records the class responses on chart paper.

6. After the discussion, the students fill in the final sections of the graphic organizers, describing how their thinking changed as a result of the activity. The teacher facilitates the students' discussion as they complete this section.

7. Student pairs then pose their own questions regarding the reading. Each partner responds to the other's questions, and the pair repeats the process with the graphic organizer.

An Application of the Think–Pair–Share Strategy for Grade 4

It is early May and Ms. Horner has assigned *Harry Potter and the Chamber of Secrets*, by J. K. Rowling (2000) as their last literature study unit. The students are avid fans of the *Harry Potter* series, and Ms. Horner has decided to use their interest to keep the class engaged during the last few weeks of the academic

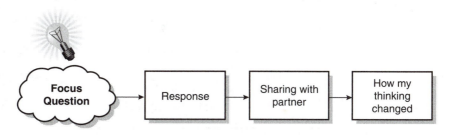

FIGURE 5.13: Sample Graphic Organizer

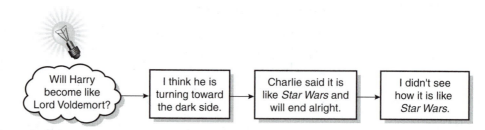

FIGURE 5.14: James's Graphic Organizer

year. She presents to the class this focus question: "Will Harry Potter become more like Voldemort?"

James and Tommy enthusiastically complete their own individual graphic organizers before they share their responses. James's graphic organizer is shown in Figure 5.14. After the reading partners have shared their responses, Ms. Horner compiles the class's statements about how their thinking changed on the chart shown in Figure 5.15. In order to complete the literature unit, Ms. Horner asks the students to write down their predictions for the next *Harry Potter* text. The students' responses will be used for the next Think–Pair–Share lesson.

Assessment Procedure

The Annotated Checklist for the Think–Pair–Share strategy (Figure 5.16) can be used to evaluate a student's performance during the activity.

Step by Step

1. The teacher observes the student's behaviors throughout the activity to offer feedback to him or her. The teacher offers feedback on the assessment data during individual conferences so that students can improve their performance.

2. Students rate their own performances.
   a. *Proficient:* Consistently demonstrates mastery of the benchmark behavior; experiences no difficulties and needs no assistance from others.
   b. *Developing:* Does not consistently demonstrate mastery of the benchmark behavior; demonstrates mastery for the majority of tasks, but needs assistance for others.
   c. *Beginning:* Rarely demonstrates mastery of the benchmark behavior; often needs assistance from others.

HOW OUR THINKING CHANGED

1. Now many students think Harry will be turning toward the dark side.

2. Now we see similar plots to other stories and myths.

3. We also changed our predictions about Harry's future.

FIGURE 5.15: Think–Pair–Share

Annotated Checklist for Think–Pair–Share Strategy

Name _____   Date _____

Critical-Thinking Behaviors	Beginning	Developing	Proficient
Summarizes content and identifies main idea.			
Identifies main idea.			
Elaborates and develops ideas with supporting details.			
Identifies metacognitive strategies to use during reading.			
Responds to critical-thinking question and shares it with partner.			
Works collaboratively with partner to generate common response.			
Works collaboratively to generate critical-thinking questions.			

SUMMARY OF PERFORMANCE

FIGURE 5.16: Annotated Checklist for the Think–Pair–Share Strategy

3. The teacher may choose to distribute assessment forms to the whole class for feedback from their peers, as well. The assessment form may also be used by students to self-evaluate their work.

Professional Resources to Explore

Ennis, R. H. (1996). *Critical thinking.* Upper Saddle River, NJ: Prentice Hall.

Luke, A. (2001). Critical literacy in Australia: A matter of context and standpoint. *Journal of Adult and Adolescent Literacy, 43*(5), 448–461.

Sibberson, F., & Szymusiak, K. (2004). *Bringing reading to life: Instruction and conversation, grades 3–6.* Portland, ME: Stenhouse.

References

Armbruster, B. B., & Osborn, J. H. (2002). *Reading instruction and assessment: Understanding the IRA Standards.* Boston, MA: Allyn & Bacon.

Garner, R., Hare, V. C., Alexander, P., Haynes, J., & Winograd, P. (1984). Inducing use of a text lookback strategy among unsuccessful readers. *American Educational Research Journal, 21,* 789–798.

Goldenberg, C. (1996). Latin American immigration and U.S. schools. *Social Policy Report of the Society for Research in Child Development, 10*(1), 1–29.

Hansen, J., & Pearson, P. D. (1983). An instructional study: Improving the inferential comprehension of fourth grade good and poor readers. *Journal of Educational Psychology, 75,* 821–829.

National Reading Panel. (2000). *Teaching children to read: An evidence-based assessment of the scientific research literature on reading and its implications for reading instruction.* Washington, DC: National Institute of Child Health and Human Development.

Rogoff, B. (1995). Observing sociocultural activity on three planes: Participatory appropriation, guided participation and apprenticeship. In J. V. Wertsch, P. DelRio, & A. Alvarez (Eds.), *Sociocultural studies of mind* (pp. 139–164). New York: Cambridge University Press.

Unrau, N. (2004). *Content area reading and writing: Fostering literacies in middle and high school cultures.* Upper Saddle River, NJ: Pearson.

Vygotsky, L. S. (1962). *Thought and language.* Cambridge: MIT Press.

Children's Literature Reference

Rowling, J. K. (1998). *Harry Potter and the chamber of secrets.* New York: Scholastic.

INDEX

report writing, 171–175

research (gathering/organization information), 171–175

Rey, H. A., 101–102

Rosenblatt, L., 2, 34

Routman, R., 122

Rowling, J. K., 4, 178, 187–188

rubrics (for assessment of)

argument development, 182, 184

creative story writing, 130, 131

critical thinking, 175, 182, 184

discussion skills, 152, 153

oral story retelling, 16, 17, 42–44

research, 175

story elements, 42–44, 98

vocabulary acquisition, 59, 60, 74, 76

writing, 92–93, 97–99, 101, 102, 103, 107, 108, 130, 131, 135–137

Ryder, R. J., 167

scaffolding, 34, 121, 126. *See also* prior knowledge

schemata, 24, 34

self-assessment (of)

argument development, 185

characterization skills, 179

comprehension skills, 5, 52, 53

critical-thinking skills, 152, 179–180, 185, 188, 189

discussion skills, 143, 144, 147, 148, 149, 152

independent reading, 52, 53

journal writing, 114

oral language skills, 99, 143, 144

reading logs and, 52

reading, 52, 143, 144

writing, 94, 99, 102, 114

self-selected books, 51. *See also* independent reading

Semantic Mapping strategy, 72–77

Sendak, M., 35–36

sentence strips, 57, 58

shared book experience, 57

Shared Pen strategy, 121–124

shared reading, 105

shared writing, 121–124

Silverstein, S., 69

simulated journals, 112–113. *See also* journals

Sketch-to-Stretch strategy, 29–33

Snowy Day, The (Keats), 58–59

Socratic Seminar strategy, 159–164

special-needs students

critical-thinking skills of, 182

discussion skills of, 142, 143, 155, 159

reading skills of, 34

stance (and reading comprehension), 2, 29–33, 34

story comprehension. *See* comprehension

story elements, 39–44

assessment of, 42–44, 98, 136

characterization. *See* characterization

comprehension and, 8–13, 14, 15, 18–23, 39–44, 45–49

content, 39, 125

creative story writing and, 125–131

graphic organizers and, 39–44

plot, 15–16, 18–23, 39, 127

resolution, 39

setting, 15, 39

story maps/mapping and, 19, 39–44, 133

story pyramids and, 19, 45–49

story retelling and, 132–137

structure, 15–16, 39, 45, 125

understanding of, 8–13, 14, 15–16, 18–19, 20, 39, 98, 125

writing and, 98, 125–131

story excitement, 18. *See also* story tension

Story Impressions strategy, 125–131

Story Mapping strategy, 39–44. *See also* story maps/mapping

story maps/mapping

assessment and, 41–44

description of, 39

English language learners and, 133

examples of, 35, 41, 42, 134

story elements and, 19, 39–44, 133

story retelling and, 34, 35–36, 39, 40, 41–44, 132–137

Story Pyramids strategy, 45–49

story retelling

assessment and, 16, 17, 42–44, 132

comprehension and, 14–17, 35, 36–37, 39, 40, 41–44

drawing and, 132

narrative text and, 14–17, 35, 36–37

oral approach to, 14–17, 35, 36–37, 39, 40, 41–44

props used in, 14, 15, 16

story elements and, 132–137

story maps/mapping and, 34, 35–36, 39, 40, 41–44, 132–137

written approach to, 132–137

story schema, 45. *See also* story elements

story tension, 18–23. *See also* plot

story writing, 125–131. *See also* writing

Storyboards strategy, 34–38

strategic readers, 34. *See also* prior knowledge; schemata

struggling readers/writers

comprehension of, 34

content-area knowledge of, 182

critical-thinking skills of, 182, 186

discussion skills of, 151, 155, 156